Central Banks and Economic Indicators

Forex Fundamental Analysis

DAVID CARLI

First Printing: 2017

ISBN: 9798670643658

Website: www.tradingwithdavid.com
E-mail: info@tradingwithdavid.com

EDITED

Caroline Winter
carolinewinter4@hotmail.com

CONTENTS

ABOUT THE AUTHOR

INTRODUCTION

David Carli is an Italian trader and independent financial analyst. He completed his studies at the University of Pisa, and since then he has released several successful books about trading. It is his success and knowledge that David wishes to pass on to other potential traders, helping them to avoid mistakes so that they might succeed in the finance and investment markets.

After completing his studies at the University of Pisa, David attended several exclusive trading courses run and organised by Steve Nison in the United States of America. David believes that the best person to manage your investments is yourself. Only you can understand how long and hard you had to work to achieve your savings. By helping you avoid the strategies that do not work, David hopes to give all traders a better chance at success.

Since January 2007, David has been living and working as a full-time trader. It was during 2007 that David began collaborating with several highly-placed trading websites and magazines. During the financial crisis of 2008, David learned the importance of diversification in trading, helping to achieve low-risk investments. David studied the best approach across all markets to achieve a balanced asset allocation of savings.

In 2012 and 2013 David worked for a small Italian Fund, but in January 2014 he left to manage his investments on a full-time basis. In 2018, He started to collaborate with an important European commodity investment company.

He is currently also working on several books for those that wish to learn more about certain aspects of trading such as Forex, options, commodity and spread trading, stocks, and more. David also teaches interested investors his personal trading strategies and how to apply them in different markets.

He hopes that through books, courses, videos, and articles, people will better understand the financial markets and investment sectors. On https://tradingwithdavid.com, you will also find David's analyses and his trades made using his strategies. You will see that each aspect of his trades is always well planned and thought out.

ABOUT TRADINGVIEW

INTRODUCTION

TradingView is the innovative financial platform created by Multicharts for the web browsing market, in order to bring the tools that were once only granted to institutional and investment funds, to a much wider audience, free of charge.

The peculiarity of this platform is the way it flanks the charts with a social component, where users share their trading ideas to compare themselves with others and improve together.

To create even more chemistry between traders, there are public chats, where users exchange opinions in real-time on the latest market movements.

The prerogative of TradingView is that not being a broker, it is not limited to providing only its market data. On the contrary, it plays a sort of role as a hub where more than 50 providers spread all over the world are collected and where quotes and charts can be consulted.

About the platform, it is difficult to describe the ease and immediacy with which the charts respond. This is because TradingView has developed a proprietary, JavaScript-based programming language called PineScript, which lets anyone develop their own customised financial analysis tools. The company "freemium" offer a software as a service model that lets most users connect and exchange trading tips and tricks for free.

Personalization is truly the greatest aspect of this platform. Every single instrument can be customised, and every detail can be modified.

You can use all types of charts, over 100 ready-to-use indicators, and over 5000 scripts provided by the developer community that populates TradingView. You can build spreads and compare two or more charts.

TradingView lets you discover investment ideas and showcase your talents to a large and active community of traders. Freely discuss, share, and learn with thousands of market participants using TradingView.

With TradingView, the sky is the limit.

PREFACE

INTRODUCTION

Forex is the most exciting and dynamic market. With its 4 trillion dollars traded each day, it is the largest financial market in the world, and that's why it is also the one that causes the most speculation.

Trading with currencies is very easy, all you have to do is Google search, and you will find a flood of brokers with which to open an account, usually with a few Dollars. What is not so easy is getting constant profits every month.

With "Forex with Fundamental Analysis" you will discover a new way of seeing the Forex, and of analysing a currency pair. You will learn the dynamics that really move currencies.

You will understand the motivations behind specific movements; you will get a clear analysis of each currency, and you will know how to use it to your advantage. It is not certainly an indicator that makes a currency pair rise or fall, but a much larger force.

You will learn a correct and well-defined method to trade a currency pair. You will follow the trail of the big speculators, by distancing yourself from the mass of small fish that every day get eaten by sharks that swim in the "forex ocean."

A method that comes from over 25 years of experience in financial markets, as well as my expertise as a fund manager of a small Italian investment bank, and which I perfected and made possible for use by all traders.

At first glance, probably some concepts may seem complicated, but I assure you that with time and practice you will assimilate them without any problems, and it will become natural to apply them in your forex analysis.

You just have to stop seeing a currency pair as a single entity, like a price, and start, instead, to see it as two opposing economies because a currency is the mirror of its economy. You do not have to see Eur-Usd as a single market, but as the Eurozone economy versus the American economy.

This concept is the starting point of the entire analysis that you will learn reading this book. A book that took me, from the first to the last edition, about four years to write. This is because my experience grew, and consequently, the topics covered increased and improved.

"Forex with Fundamental Analysis" is a book that will change your way of trading in the forex market. With its modest price, it is my gift for all those who aspire to become professional traders.

For any question, do not hesitate to contact me at the e-mail address info@tradingwithdavid.com, it will be my pleasure to answer all of you. Also, visit my website https://tradingwithdavid.com, where you will find free articles, analyses, and books.

THE HISTORY OF FOREX

CHAPTER 1

Forex or FX stands for "Foreign Exchange" or exchange of foreign currency, the currency purchased by travellers when visiting another country. For example, we can sell Dollars and buy Euros to travel to an EU nation (i.e. France, Portugal, or Italy). But the online Forex market is 90% speculative, which means that the operator does not take possession of the actual currency, in physical form, but opens and closes trades making a profit or loss which is then recorded on the online account.

The currency market owes its existence to the abandonment in 1971 of the Bretton Woods agreements and the ensuing collapse of the fixed exchange rate regime. In 1967, a bank in Chicago refused to give a loan in Pound Sterling to Milton Friedman, a college professor, because he intended to use these funds to sell the British currency.

Friedman, who had perceived that the pound was overvalued against the Dollar, wanted to sell the currency, and then repay the bank after the pound depreciation, thus pocketing a quick profit. The refusal of the bank to give the loan was due to the Bretton Woods agreements, established twenty-three years before, fixing the value of the national currency against the Dollar, and the Dollar exchange rate at a value of $ 45 per ounce of gold.

The Bretton Woods agreement was signed in 1944 to introduce international monetary stability in order to prevent the flight of capital abroad among the various nations and to restrict speculation on currencies. Before the agreement, between 1876 and the First World War, the gold trade was prevalent and dominated the international economic system.

During this period, the currencies acquired a new phase of stability; the price of gold reinforced them. It was abolished due to the fact that the old practice, used by kings and rulers arbitrarily, devalued the money and triggered inflation. But, the standardisation of the gold exchange had its flaws. As the economy grew stronger, imports from abroad quickly increased, causing a drop in gold reserves that were needed to print money.

As a result, the money supply reduced, the interest rates levitated, and the economic activity decreased until the recession limit. Finally, the prices of goods touched rock-bottom. This depreciation attracted purchases from other nations, which gave rise to a fever of purchases that were injected into the gold economy, bringing down interest rates which in turn revitalised the health of the economy.

This rapid economic expansion prevailed during this period until the First World War which interrupted the flow of trade and the free movement of goods. After the wars, the Agreement of Breton Woods was signed, and the participating countries agreed to maintain the value of their currency within a narrow margin against the Dollar and the corresponding value of gold as needed.

In various countries, it was forbidden to devalue their currency to benefit their businesses and they were allowed to do so only in a devaluation minor than 10%.

In the 50s, the increasing expansion of trade volumes led to massive movements of capital generated by post-war reconstruction. All of this destabilised the exchange rates that were set in Bretton Woods. The Agreement was finally abandoned in 1971 when the US unilaterally left the Bretton Woods agreements, and the US Dollar was no longer convertible into gold.

Since 1973, the currencies of major industrialised nations have begun to float freely, controlled mainly by supply and demand in the Forex market. The daily fluctuation of prices, the increase in sales volume and price volatility in the 70s, gave rise to a new financial instrument, the market deregulation and liberalisation of trade.

In 1978, following the second major devaluation of the US Dollar, the fixed exchange rate mechanism was resigned entirely from the US government and replaced with a floating exchange rate. This floating exchange rate, in turn, has been adopted by the other major currencies, turning them into a good whose value fluctuated because of the force of supply and demand.

This free-floating exchange rate between all the currencies of the world was the birth of the International foreign exchange market. In the '80s, with the advent of computers and technology, the movement of capital in the international arena has greatly accelerated extending in a continuous market through the Asian, European and American time slots.

These same technologies have made it possible for private investors to enter this market traditionally dominated only by banks and institutions. Transactions in the Forex grew from about 70 billion dollars a day in the 80s, to more than 4 trillion a day in the next three decades, with about 90% of the volumes traded for speculative purposes.

There have been several radical changes in the world economy in recent decades. Some of these changes have reduced barriers, and increased opportunities in world trade: the fall of communism in the Soviet Union and Eastern Europe, the renewed political reform in South America and the continued liberalisation of the economy of China have launched the world economy by opening new markets and new opportunities. These events have upped their traditional trade barriers resulting in a tremendous increase in international investments.

With this increase, all nations are more interrelated and dependent on each other. The increased trade and international investment have led the economic activities more and more to a greater interrelationship.

Fluctuations in the economic activity of a country are reflected in the currency of that country and are immediately forwarded to the commercial partners, alters the prices of its products and thus affecting costs and profits, which in turn affect the rate of currency exchange.

The reports of routinely disclosed economic data around the world, such as inflation, unemployment levels, as well as natural disasters or political instability, altering the convenience of owning a particular currency, and affect the international supply or demand of that particular currency. The Forex market is, in general, vital to the prosperity of the free world economy.

Every single day currencies are bought and sold to the value of over $4 trillion. It is by far the market with the most daily transactions. This volume of transactions is equivalent to about four months of trading on the New York Stock Exchange (NYSE), which has an average daily value traded of 45 million Dollars. Forex is, in essence, 100 times larger than the NYSE.

Unfortunately, from 1971 until a few years ago, the owners of this market were the major banks, brokers and the big multinational corporations, and the only way to access it, for an individual investor, was to rely on banks who demanded a minimum of one million Dollar cash deposit. Also, the sophisticated technology of communication and trading needed were not yet within the reach of most individuals.

The great revolution there was with the advent of the internet: they are born, so, the Forex online brokers that allow everyone to operate in the currency market with just a PC connected to the internet.

Introduction to Forex

Chapter 2

When we go to treat the Forex, we go to address scenarios that directly affect our lives. For example, we purchase a product that is built outside the monetary area of belonging. The final price of this product is not only affected by the production costs but will also be important in the evaluation of the exchange rate, which ultimately can result in savings for the purchaser, but runs the risk of increasing the costs.

The relationships between different currencies affect all international trade. A peculiarity of this market is, therefore, the opening and closing times. We are used to the standard stock exchange markets, which have restricted times which open and close daily. On the contrary, there is an opening in the Forex on Sundays at 5 pm which then gets closed on Friday at 5 pm (Eastern Time). This is because, as mentioned above, the currency market affects all international trade and could not be restricted to certain hours.

Having the possibility for the Forex to be open at all hours also creates an additional path to the development of our analysis. We can see the overlap of the zones of the different financial centres that produces an increase of volatility at intersections (figure 1).

FOREX MARKETS																								
AM												PM												
1	2	3	4	5	6	7	8	9	10	11	12	1	2	3	4	5	6	7	8	9	10	11	12	
		LONDON																						
					NEW YORK																			
																SYDNEY								
																		TOKYO						

Figure 1 - The Forex Trading Hours

As we can see, the large and most interesting overlap occurs between the London market, the most important in Europe, and New York. During this period, the volatility increases dramatically due to a large number of operators that influence the supply and demand of the various currencies. So, the probability of having high volatility during the overlap of the two financial centres (London and New York) is very high.

The one between London and New York is not the only overlap; there are also those of Sydney and Tokyo and Tokyo and London.

The lack of a physical headquarters in Forex with predefined times of daily opening and closing makes it OTC; meaning an Over-The-Counter market. Trading takes place directly between two parties without going through the exchange. In this way, we can easily access the online virtual market anywhere in the world.

As mentioned in the previous chapter, the Forex market is the largest and most liquid in the world, with over 4 trillion in daily trading. Trades are 90%

speculative and generated not only by the large investors and investment banks but also by private investors with small capital through **leverage**.

For example, if we invest with leverage of 1:100, we invest 1 of equity, but we manage, we work, and we get the results on a capital of 100. The leverage, then, is a double-edged sword because our profits, but also our losses, are multiplied compared to our real investment. It is a plus that offers us the market, but only if we use it well do we get the benefits.

Another important aspect regarding the Forex is that it is **bi-directional**, that is, we have the opportunity to get a profit both upward and downward.

In the Forex market, we are going to buy and sell a currency compared with another one (currency pair). So, when we buy a currency pair, we buy the **base currency** (the first), and we sell the **quote currency** (the second). When, instead, we sell a currency pair, we sell the base currency, and we buy the quote currency.

For example, if we decide to sell USD-CAD, all we do with our operation is to sell US Dollars and buy Canadian Dollars. If we buy EUR-JPY, we are purchasing Euros and selling Japanese Yen.

To close the trade that we have opened, we have to do the opposite of the previous trade. If, for example, we have bought Euro and sold British pounds and we want to close the trade, we have to buy in equal measure English Pounds and sell Euro in order to have a balanced net position. An operation that is done directly from the trading platform when we give the order to close the trade.

In the Forex market, there are eight major currencies which make up 80% of trade. Seven of these currencies, coupled with the eighth, the US Dollar (USD), form the so-called "**Majors**." They are:

EUR/USD, USD/CHF, GPB/USD, USD/JPY, USD/CAD, AUD/USD, NZD/USD.

Currency pairs that do not contain the US Dollar are known as **Cross-Currency Pairs** or only "**Crosses**." Historically, if we wanted to convert a currency, we would first have to convert the currency into US Dollars and then into the currency which we desired.

With the introduction of the Crosses, we no longer have to do this tedious calculation as all brokers now offer the direct exchange rates. The most active crosses are derived from the three major non-US Dollar currencies (Euro, UK Pound and Japanese Yen). These currency pairs are also known as **Minors**. An example:

EUR/JPY, EUR/GBP, EUR/CHF, AUD/NZD, NZD/JPY, GBP/JPY, AUD/JPY, GBP/CAD etc.

In the end, there are the "**Exotics**" that are made up of a major currency paired with the one of an emerging or a strong but smaller economy from a global perspective, such as Singapore, South Africa or European countries outside of the Eurozone.

These currency pairs are not traded as often as the majors or crosses, so the cost for making trading with these currency pairs can be higher, due to the lack of liquidity in these markets. An example:

USD/SGD, EUR/SEK, USD/RUB, EUR/TRY, USD/ZAR, EUR/DKK, USD/NOK, USD/MXN etc.

The major players in the Forex market are the Central Banks, investment banks, institutional investors and hedge funds which, thanks to their financial capabilities, move the entire market. With them, in recent years, aided also by the advent of the internet, have been added the private investors (retail) as well. They are, however, a tiny part, from the point of view of the capital held, compared to the big banks or hedge funds.

Precisely because these retail investors are so small, they become, for the big speculators, preys, with the possibility of being hunted. The most novice traders without any experience suffer their losses because they are focused on the wrong things within the market. So, they make errors due to lack of experience, such as a wrong position size.

How do we pass from being a hunted prey to a trader who follows what the large investors do, to thus become profitable over time? At the start of my trader life, I tried many strategies, but most of them had limits in practice. They were based on tools (indicators) that, in turn, were based on a mathematical calculation, however that they could not evaluate the evolution of the market. I was facing the evolution of a market (Forex, equities, commodity, etc.) always seeing it in the same way.

An example of this would be if a person dressed all year in the same manner. But the seasons change and there are colder and warmer days. The same is true in the Forex and in trading in general. How would an indicator address these situations? Always in the same way, because it is based on unchanging statistical and mathematical calculations. So, it may not be the most appropriate method for all situations that arise when we operate in the markets.

How can we, therefore, approach this market and be profitable, having at least the statistics on our side? By working in the currency market, getting some important benchmarks. I am talking about the Central Banks (which we will see in one of the next chapters), the real market makers in Forex which move in a realistic way the value of the individual economies, (not speculative).

Whenever there are the central banks' meetings, these capture the attention of all the major players, and they generate data that are the mirrors of the true potential of individual economies. They give essential input and fundamental boundaries to distinguish what is the real strength of individual currencies from what is speculation.

These considerations are based on the method that we will see explained later, which allows me to manage my portfolio. Not only with the currencies but also with other instruments linked to Forex market (such as options). It is crucial to have definite detailed plans and always knowing how to behave in every situation without falling prey to emotions which are often bad counsellors.

TECHNICAL VS. FUNDAMENTAL
CHAPTER 3

Fundamental analysis and technical analysis represent the two different approaches to which reference can be made when we trade in Forex (and not only). The first has to do with the so-called fundamentals of the economy, and then with the essentially economic aspects of the issue, while the second focuses particularly on the price movements of a currency pair to intuit and predict its subsequent movements.

Both fundamental analysis and technical analysis are useful in Forex: the two approaches can also be used together, for analysing financial market trends satisfactorily and profitably.

Technical Analysis

Technical analysis is the study of price trends with the use of charts. The interest of a technical analyst is to look for the graphics configurations that are drawn by price movements. The market trend is evaluated to understand possible future price movements.

The pure technical analysis is not based on any fundamental of the underlying asset but applies a series of technical tools drawn on the chart, to allow the prediction of future movements.

The tools available to a trader who wants to achieve this goal are many: among these, there are the trading indicators, which are specific mathematical formulas that represent the factors that affect the price of a particular asset from a graphical point of view. A technical analyst can understand, only by looking at the charts, in the short-term, medium-term or long-term, whether a currency pair is destined to fall or rise.

There are a lot of indicators used by technical analysts to try to predict the next price movements. One of the most used indicators is the "simple moving average", which is calculated on a certain amount of price data and is mobile because it moves from period to period. Given an average of a certain time-frame, the most recent data is added each time, eliminating the last data in the series from the calculation.

The moving average can be used as a watershed between bullish and bearish trend, or dynamic support or resistance (a concept that we will explore further later on in this book).

Fundamental Analysis

When we talk about fundamental analysis, we refer to the discipline that focuses not on price charts but the so-called macro-economy, that is to say, the part of the economy that has to do with the forecasts on fundamental factors.

The price evolution of a currency pair, in fact, also depends on political events, economic crises, wars, acquisitions of companies and multinationals, the news published on specialised media, market rumours and so on. Based on this approach, therefore, traders have the opportunity to understand and know the economic aspects on which price development depend and then exploit them and make money.

The first difference between fundamental analysis and technical analysis is that for the first analyst, it is necessary to examine balances, data and statistics, whilst the second refers essentially to charts.

Hence, a fundamental analyst focuses on economic theory and related accounting, econometric and statistical methods: it is an approach that, as we can guess, is based on a longer period of time compared to the horizon of technical analysis.

The technical analysis, to be honest, can be set to different time-frames, a few minutes or even years: fundamental analysis, however, has not the same freedom of choice, as the data must be interpreted over time. Fundamental analysis and technical analysis, in essence, are concepts and almost opposite ways of understanding Forex, but it does not mean that they cannot coexist: in fact, several traders combine them in their analyses.

For example, the tools of technical analysis can be useful to a fundamental analyst to give him the opportunity to understand when is the most suitable time for the market entry (the timing). On the other hand, a technical analyst can decide to use, in addition to technical signals, also the economic fundamentals, to understand if the suggestion to buy or sell that can come from a pattern on a chart is also supported by the fundamental data.

At this point, there is nothing left to do but to examine the other differences and the other characteristics of the two types of analysis, starting from the importance of timing: this element, which is very significant for a successful trader, can be understood as the best time for the market entry. With the right timing, the stop-loss is closer, which means higher odds of success and reduction in losses.

The study of the charts (and therefore, the technical analysis) allows us to understand the key levels of the timing. Another factor that deserves to be taken into consideration is that, sometimes, an event can already be priced into the market or price. In the sense that, fundamental analysis is incorporated into the technical analysis. In other words, within the charts are often priced all the elements of fundamental analysis (the ones we mentioned earlier: political events, economic crises, and so on).

Furthermore, it is worth pointing out that the fundamental analysis is less flexible than the technical analysis, which allows one to focus on stop-losses and, above all, to program the various objectives for the most different time-frames.

Last but not least is the aspect that has to do with ease of finding information. Once, finding news and data was very complicated, especially for a common investor. Nowadays, thanks to the advent of the internet, anyone can find all the data and news to carry out a complete analysis. And that is what we will see later.

However, we must not make the mistake of believing that for long-term investments, we must opt for fundamental analysis, while for short-term investments, we must opt for technical analysis. A division into watertight compartments of this type is neither fruitful nor correct since, with the appropriate measures and adequate knowledge, both the techniques can be useful in the short, medium and long-term.

So, which of the two methods to use? Maybe a combination of both?

Let me tell you a secret (which is not, in point of fact, all that secret). I worked for an Italian investment bank for two years, managing a small fund.

In an investment bank, nobody uses technical analysis. No indicator or oscillator is used; the same is the case for Fibonacci, Gann or Elliott. The only thing traders of an investment bank look at is the fundamentals.

The only way to earn in trading is to increase your skills. No system makes you earn money automatically... otherwise, do not you think that big investment banks would use it instead of paying hundreds of traders?

You have to learn the fundamental logics, do not trade by looking at the charts. When you trade, it is necessary to study the reasons that drive the prices, what moves them.

And this is what you will learn in this book: to trade currencies like an investment bank.

INSIDE A CURRENCY PAIR

CHAPTER 4

We are used to taking a currency pair, for example, Eur-Usd, and seeing it as a single market, as a price. This is wrong. Instead, we have to see it in a completely different way. We have to go behind the scenes and understand the dynamics, how the currency pair is formed. Because by doing this, we will understand better and better how to treat it and exploit it to our advantage.

So, we must learn to see this currency pair as splitting the two variables, similar to spread trading. Eur-Usd, we should not see as a single market, but as two combined economies; the Eurozone economy and the US one. Just doing each other's analysis of the economies, we can grasp aspects of strength and weakness that then, in the context of the time, they can come to develop.

If we take stock, such as Facebook, and look at its chart and movements, this is related to the company (i.e., if Facebook releases earnings lower than expected, the stock fall even though the Nasdaq index will gain a lot). So, why do we have to look at the Eur-Usd and treat it as the Facebook one? On the one hand, we are talking to an individual company, here comprising of two economies. So, logically, we cannot treat them in the same way. There are roads to be taken very differently, and this is what I am going to delve into.

Because, whether we like it or not, we will need Forex forever if we trade. Do we trade with commodities? With spread trading? With options (mainly in the US market)? We will gain and lose Dollars, but in Europe, there is the Euro, the Canadian Dollar in Canada, in Australia, the Australian Dollar, etc. Hence, to know the Forex dynamics for managing foreign exchange risks will be for us very, very useful.

Often, we hear about correlations (I will talk about it in a later chapter). Within Forex, the correlation between an economy and a commodity are interesting because the price of raw material may heavily influence an economy (and we will see it better in the chapter about "Commodity Currencies").

An aspect we are going to see and that I find significant is the "Safe-Haven Currencies." When we speak of safe-haven assets, we always talk about gold and silver, but we can cover ourselves and extend the protection of our portfolio, even with some currencies such as the Swiss Franc and the Japanese Yen.

We will explore safe-haven currencies in more depth in a subsequent chapter. When we work with currencies it is crucial to always remember that this market was created primarily for international trade.

So, within this market, there is a vastness to it that is immense. We are used to seeing it, such as speculative operations, with enormous leverage. We should instead see it in its primary nature, that of coverage. Leverage is just a "game" invented to induce more people to work in this market (try going to Apple and buying an iPhone with $ 20 with the leverage effect...).

Those of you that worked with high leverage got to see what happened at the beginning of 2015 with the Swiss Franc, and how much you can really lose with this "little game." Very often the Forex is seen in this way, a game, not because it is a market from which to stay away, but because many brokers have given it powerful leverage and it can be traded with very little money. But a powerful leverage effect is not only useful in getting a profit; we can lose a lot as well.

This is what often happens in the Forex market, and this is why so many people lose a lot of money on the Forex, maybe even more than in other markets. The reality is that if Forex is handled in the right way, we can acknowledge and adequately handle the risks involved, in order for it to become a good market for us to exploit.

CENTRAL BANKS

CHAPTER 5

As I previously mentioned, the biggest market maker that moves the currency market is the central bank, but what is a central bank?

The central bank is a public institution that manages the currency of a country or group of countries and controls the money supply, literally, the amount of money in circulation. The main objective of many central banks is price stability. In some countries, central banks are also required by law to act in support of full employment.

One of the main tools of any central bank is setting interest rates, the "cost of money", as part of its monetary policy. The central bank is not a commercial bank. An individual cannot open an account in a central bank or ask it for a loan and, as a public body, it is not motivated by profit.

Supply and demand are the underlying logic that moves a currency pair, and these are made by those that hold a certain richness, and who are those that hold riches if not the central banks? It is not the technical analysis that moves a market, an indicator in the overbought or oversold zone. There are completely different elements within the economy.

The logic of working in the medium to long-term is not to know so much a pattern but the thoughts of those who move these currencies and the economies.

From their directives, therefore, large investors take their trading decisions. Besides, who may have the power if not the one who decides whether or not to cut or raise interest rates? Who builds money creation programs? Who adopts policies to extend or narrow the value of the individual economies and, consequently, the weight of their currencies?

Their decisions can drastically move the foundations of an economy and, above all, can influence the development in the following months. Accordingly, we can take advantage of these situations exactly as the big investors do (the investment banks).

Figure 2 - Eur-Usd weekly chart (TradingView.com)

Let's take a look at an example to gain a better understanding of this. In figure 2 above, we can see the Eur-Usd weekly chart. On January 22, 2015, it was announced, at an ECB meeting, the asset purchase program, the QE (Quantitative Easing). Namely, the Euro currency injection in the market.

The announcement of the QE program introduction caused a drop of Eur-Usd from about 1.1600 to a price that has come to hit 1.1115 in less than 24 hours.

By using several conventional indicators, many traders (I personally know some of them) saw the opportunity to enter, but in a bullish direction, after the first bearish wave on January 22, thus creating an opportunity for large investors to make the currency pair on January 23 come down still further, blasting all the strategies that traders tend to use, limited only by a graphic analysis or certain types of static indicators and unsupported by the point of view of great economic trends.

Forex and the markets, in general, do not only have the technical levels but also "fundamental levels." In the chart the level of 1.1600, as we have seen, is the value of Eur-Usd when Mario Draghi announced the Quantitative Easing (QE), where it was formed a "fundamental resistance." Exceeding that level would be to deny everything that is the macroeconomic environment created by the ECB.

Important. Keep in mind that in the markets as in life, everything is possible. So, I am not saying it is impossible to exceed 1.1600, because if the medium to long-term central banks move the currencies, the short-time enables speculation to do it. However, it is a significant level, and therefore not easy to overcome. This will be the case until conditions change.

So, when we go to think about building large positions against the market makers, we have to consider the idea of putting ourselves in opposition to someone much stronger and bigger than us.

It is important to consider what moves to make in order to gain a statistical advantage resulting from those who hold power (central banks), compared to the indicators and all the offerings landscape in the world of trading.

Now, to conclude this chapter, let's see what the main Central Banks are.

- United States: **Federal Reserve (Fed)**
- Canada: **Bank of Canada (BoC)**
- Eurozone: **European Central Bank (ECB)**
- Great Britain: **Bank of England (BoE)**
- Switzerland: **Swiss National Bank (SNB)**
- Japan: **Bank of Japan (BoJ)**
- Australia: **Reserve Bank of Australia (RBA)**
- New Zealand: **Reserve Bank of New Zealand (RBNZ)**
- China: **People's Bank of China (PBoC)**

These are all the real market makers in the financial markets in general. In their sites we can find and read the reports and minutes of the various meetings.

These turn out to be really important in building and revising our operational plans. In or by creating the synthesis schemes for each currency, we can get a complete macroeconomic overview that can help us in many situations.

Constructing a scheme with all the most important news and macroeconomic data is also the method used by traders who work in the investment banks. Why? Because, as I mentioned, they do not move the money because an indicator is in the overbought or oversold zone but where the shark is, and the largest sharks are the central banks, those who have the most money. They are the ones who run the entire economy, pulling the strings.

One word from them, good or bad, can create a strong movement, and we know that the world of currencies affects directly and indirectly throughout the rest of the financial landscape. Understanding the currency becomes crucial to avoiding unpleasant situations in other markets. For example, commodities are traded in US Dollars, and therefore, the value of the Dollar tends to influence them (e.g., a Dollar too strong is negative for the commodities).

Important. It is not uncommon for a decision to be announced days or weeks before by the central bank chairman. So, often, the decisions have already been priced into the market.

LONG-TERM TRADING

CHAPTER 6

To understand this type of trading, we must start with the concept of trading with a long-term goal, where operations have the capacity to remain latent for several months, only to then try and express the real values of the economies to which they refer.

I practically do not use technical analysis. I take into account only the static supports and resistances given by volumes when I have to decide the market entry. In my trading, in the management of my money, I have always tried to reproduce, as far as I could do it, the work done when I was a fund manager. As I already said, fundamental analysis is only used in an investment bank.

The first step, which must become a procedure, it is to go to subdivide the legs that form the currency pair. Let us remember that the currency pairs are all relations. We have to analyse each leg (each currency, so, each economy), and then exploit the strengths of one and the weaknesses of the other.

Who determines the value of a company? The chair of the company. So, who is the chair of the Dollar company? The Fed. Who is the chair of the Euro company? The ECB. Thus, the central banks. We have to recognise in all this a representation of the company; we have to imagine it and see it in this context. The Dollar is a company with its Chair, Jerome Powell.

In this broader context, the first step is to divide the pros and cons of each economy by trying to define the strengths and weaknesses for both.

To clarify this concept, let's refer back to the example of Eur-Usd of the previous chapter (figure 3).

Figure 3 - Eur-Usd weekly chart (TradingView.com)

Now, we build off of summaries (February 2017) of the current state of the different economies, and we look for strengths that could give impetus to the currency, or the negative points, that would affect it, instead, in a very negative way. Let's start with **Euros**.

- Brexit
- Immigration
- Security (terrorist attacks France, Belgium, Germany)
- Political Elections in Germany, France and the Netherlands
- Extending QE = Injection of currency by the ECB
- Different economies inside
- Low Inflation

<u>Much liquidity = Devaluation of the currency (Euro)</u>

So, the European Union has the characteristics of an economy with increased liquidity in circulation and with serious structural problems.

After identifying these points regarding the Euro, so the European Union, we must develop, in the same way, the situation of the US Dollar. Following the same criteria, we have to build all the pros and cons, including future external factors that may influence the **US Dollar**.

- Domestic consumption-based economy
- Currency used for international trade
- Good jobs data
- Economy growing at a faster rate
- Three projected rate increase in 2017
- Political uncertainty caused by Donald Trump
- Problems with the budget deficit

<u>Rate increase = Even stronger Dollar</u>

The economy grows at a faster pace, but also has to deal with the Trump policy and a very strong Dollar, which damages exports.

33

So, on one side, we have the Euro economy still weak and with different problems and uncertainties. On the other hand, the US economy booming with a Fed ready to raise interest rates three times in 2017, even though it is, most of all, a manoeuvre for absorbing the huge post QE liquidity.

We have to build our scenarios and create the operating model with practical levels, where we can take advantage of market situations. It is an analysis that will lead us to a clear, definite and, most of all, real operational plan, where we will not suffer emotionally, and above all, in order to not be squashed by them.

How to build these schemes for each economy? We must split the highlights of individual currencies, we must start from the ground up, from real data and not from assumptions. To work in those situations that are tangible, where we have a real situation and not on hearsay or based on things we have read somewhere. We have to buy or sell currencies only when we have a clear situation.

And for this to happen, we must know and be able to evaluate some primary data. I will talk about this in the next chapter, which is concerned with economic indicators.

ECONOMIC INDICATORS

CHAPTER 7

Job and unemployment, GDP, consumption and inflation. These are the fields we must concentrate on when we want to get a clear and unfiltered picture of an economy.

This is because, when we read a piece of news, the author always includes, sometimes subconsciously, their own bias, thus even without intending to, we get more of an opinion than a fact or reality.

Every day, the Forex traders (as well as others) study and analyse news and macroeconomic data in order to exploit it for profit in their trading activities. When news comes out, and it creates a slight instability in currency, this currency tends to gain or lose purchasing power, that is, to gain or lose value against other currencies.

I wish to emphasise that it is not necessary to be expert economists, all we need to do is to dedicate ourself to trading, just as we would for any other job, as for any other job.

Let's see what the major and most important economic indicators are for the eight leading economies.

UNITED STATES

Non-Farm Payrolls: change in the number of employed people during the previous month, excluding the farming industry. Job creation is an important leading indicator of consumer spending, which accounts for a majority of overall economic activity. This is vital economic data released shortly after the month ends. The combination of importance and earliness makes for hefty market impacts. Released monthly, usually on the first Friday after the month ends.

Unemployment Rate: percentage of the total workforce that is unemployed and actively seeking employment during the previous month. Although it is generally viewed as a lagging indicator, the number of unemployed people is an important signal of overall economic health because consumer spending is highly correlated with labour-market conditions. Released monthly, usually on the first Friday after the month ends.

Average Hourly Earnings: change in the price businesses pay for labour, excluding the farming industry. It is a leading indicator of consumer inflation - when businesses pay more for labour, the higher costs are usually passed on to the consumer. Released monthly, usually on the first Friday after the month ends.

GDP q/q: annualised change in the inflation-adjusted value of all goods and services produced by the economy. Gross Domestic Product (GDP) is the broadest measure of economic activity and the primary gauge of the economy's health. There are three versions of GDP:

- **Advance GDP q/q**: it is the earliest and thus tends to have the most impact. Released quarterly, about 30 days after the quarter ends;

- **Prelim GDP q/q**: released quarterly, about 60 days after the quarter ends;

- **Final GDP q/q**: released quarterly, about 85 days after the quarter ends.

ISM Manufacturing PMI: level of a diffusion index based on surveyed purchasing managers, excluding the manufacturing industry. Survey of about 400 purchasing managers which asks respondents to rate the relative level of business conditions including employment, production, new orders, prices, supplier deliveries, and inventories.

It is a leading indicator of economic health when businesses react quickly to market conditions, with purchasing managers holding perhaps the most current and relevant insight into the company's view of the economy. Released monthly, on the third business day after the month ends.

CPI m/m: change in the price of goods and services purchased by consumers. CORE version: change in the price of goods and services purchased by consumers, excluding food and energy. Consumer prices account for a majority of overall inflation.

Inflation is important to currency valuation because rising prices lead the central bank to raise interest rates out of respect for their inflation containment mandate. Released monthly, about 16 days after the month ends.

PPI m/m: change in the price of finished goods and services sold by producers. The Producer Price Index (PPI) is a leading indicator of consumer inflation. When manufacturers pay more for goods, the higher costs are usually passed on to the consumer. Released monthly, about 14 days after the month ends.

Retail Sales: change in the total value of sales at the retail level. It is the primary gauge of consumer spending, which accounts for the majority of overall economic activity. Released monthly, about 13 days after the month ends.

Building Permits: annualised number of new residential building permits issued during the previous month. It is an excellent gauge of future construction activity because obtaining a permit is among the first steps in constructing a new building. Released monthly, about 17 days after the month ends.

Existing Home Sales: annualized number of residential buildings that were sold during the previous month, excluding new construction. It is a leading indicator of economic health because the sale of a home triggers a wide-reaching ripple effect. For example, renovations are done by the new owners, a mortgage is sold by the financing bank, and brokers are paid to execute the transaction. Released monthly, about 20 days after the month ends.

CANADA

Unemployment Rate: percentage of the total workforce that is unemployed and actively seeking employment during the previous month. Although it is generally viewed as a lagging indicator, the number of unemployed people is an important signal of overall economic health because consumer spending is highly correlated with labour-market conditions. Released monthly, about 8 days after the month ends.

GDP m/m: change in the inflation-adjusted value of all goods and services produced by the economy. It is the broadest measure of economic activity and the primary gauge of the economy's health. Canada is unique in that they release fresh GDP data on a monthly basis. A quarterly GDP figure is also released; however, it is merely a summation of the monthly data. Released monthly, about 60 days after the month ends.

CPI m/m: change in the price of goods and services purchased by consumers. That is the most important inflation-related release due to its earliness and broad scope. Consumer prices account for a majority of overall inflation. Inflation is important to currency valuation because rising prices lead the central bank to raise interest rates out of respect for their inflation containment mandate. Released monthly, about 20 days after the month ends.

Manufacturing Sales m/m: change in the total value of sales made by manufacturers. It is a leading indicator of economic health - manufacturers are quickly affected by market conditions, and changes in their sales can be an early signal of future activity such as spending, hiring, and investment. Released monthly, about 45 days after the month ends.

Core Retail Sales: change in the total value of sales at the retail level, excluding automobiles. Automobile sales account for about 20% of Retail Sales, but they tend to be very volatile and distort the underlying trend. The Core data is, therefore thought to be a better gauge of spending trends. Released monthly, about 50 days after the month ends.

Trade Balance: difference in value between imported and exported goods during the reported month. Export demand and currency demand are directly linked because foreigners must buy domestic currency to pay for the nation's exports.

Export demand also impacts production and prices of domestic manufacturers. A positive number indicates that more goods were exported than imported. Released monthly, about 35 days after the month ends.

EUROZONE

Unemployment Rate: percentage of the total workforce that is unemployed and actively seeking employment during the previous month. Although it is generally viewed as a lagging indicator, the number of unemployed people is an important signal of overall economic health because consumer spending is highly correlated with labour-market conditions. Released monthly, about 30 days after the month ends.

GDP q/q: change in the inflation-adjusted value of all goods and services produced by the economy. There are 3 versions of GDP released about 20 days apart – Preliminary Flash, Flash, and Revised. The Preliminary Flash release is the earliest and thus tends to have the most impact. Released quarterly, about 30 days after the quarter ends.

ZEW Economic Sentiment: level of a diffusion index based on surveyed German institutional investors and analysts. Survey of about 275 German institutional investors and analysts which asks respondents to rate the relative 6-month economic outlook for Germany.

It is a leading indicator of economic health - investors and analysts are highly informed by virtue of their job, and changes in their sentiment can be an early signal of future economic activity. Released monthly, on the second or third Tuesday of the current month.

Flash Manufacturing PMI: French, German and European level of a diffusion index based on surveyed purchasing managers in the manufacturing industry. It is a leading indicator of economic health - businesses react quickly to market conditions, and their purchasing managers hold perhaps the most current and relevant insight into the company's view of the economy.

There are 2 versions of this report released about a week apart – Flash and Final. The Flash release is the earliest and thus tends to have the most impact. Released monthly, around 3 weeks into the current month.

CPI y/y: change in the price of goods and services purchased by consumers. There are 2 versions of this report released about two weeks apart, Flash and Final. The Flash report is extremely early and tends to have a significant impact. Flash Released monthly, on the last business day of the current month.

Retail Sales m/m: change in the total value of sales at the retail level. It is the primary gauge of consumer spending, which accounts for the majority of overall economic activity. Released monthly, about 35 days after the month ends.

GREAT BRITAIN

Unemployment Rate: percentage of the total workforce that is unemployed and actively seeking employment during the previous three months. Although it is generally viewed as a lagging indicator, the number of unemployed people is an important signal of overall economic health because consumer spending is highly correlated with labour-market conditions. Released monthly, about 45 days after the month ends.

Average Earnings: change in the price businesses and the government pay for labour, including bonuses. It is a leading indicator of consumer inflation when businesses pay more for labour; the higher costs are usually passed on to the consumer. Released monthly, about 45 days after the month ends.

GDP q/q: change in the inflation-adjusted value of all goods and services produced by the economy. There are 3 versions of GDP released a month apart: Preliminary, Second Estimate, and Final.

- **The Preliminary**: it is the earliest and thus tends to have the most impact. Released quarterly, about 26 days after the quarter ends;
- **Second Estimate**: released quarterly, about 55 days after the quarter ends.
- **Final**: released quarterly, about 85 days after the quarter ends.

Manufacturing PMI: level of a diffusion index based on surveyed purchasing managers in the manufacturing industry. Survey of about 600 purchasing managers which asks respondents to rate the relative level of business conditions including employment, production, new orders, prices, supplier deliveries, and inventories. Released monthly, on the first business day after the month ends.

CPI y/y: change in the price of goods and services purchased by consumers. The average price of various goods and services are sampled and then compared to the sampling done a year earlier. Released monthly, about 16 days after the month ends.

Retail Sales: Released monthly, about 16 days after the month ends. It is the primary gauge of consumer spending, which accounts for the majority of overall economic activity. Released monthly, about 20 days after the month ends.

Construction PMI: level of a diffusion index based on surveyed purchasing managers in the construction industry. Survey of about 170 purchasing managers which asks respondents to rate the relative level of business conditions including employment, production, new orders, prices, supplier deliveries and inventories. Above 50.0 indicates industry expansion, below indicates contraction. Released monthly, on the second business day after the month ends.

Service PMI: level of a diffusion index based on surveyed purchasing managers in the services industry. Survey of purchasing managers which asks respondents to rate the relative level of business conditions including employment, production, new orders, prices, supplier deliveries and inventories. It is very important since the British economy rests heavily on services. Released monthly, on the third business day after the month ends.

SWITZERLAND

KOF Economic Research: this index is designed to predict the direction of the economy over the next 6 months. A combined reading of 219 economic indicators related to banking confidence, production, new orders, consumer confidence, exchange rate, money supply, interest rate spreads, stock market prices and housing. Released monthly, around the end of the current month.

CPI m/m: change in the price of goods and services purchased by consumers. Released monthly, about 6 days after the month ends.

PPI m/m: change in the price of goods and raw materials purchased by manufacturers. Released monthly, about 14 days after the month ends.

JAPAN

GDP q/q: change in the inflation-adjusted value of all goods and services produced by the economy. There are 2 versions of GDP release:

- **Preliminary**: it is the earliest and thus tends to have the most impact. Released quarterly, about 45 days after the quarter ends.
- **Final**: released quarterly, about 70 days after the quarter ends.

Manufacturing Index: level of a diffusion index based on surveyed large manufacturers. This survey is used to predict the BOJ's Tankan survey released about a week later. Released quarterly, about 70 days into the current quarter.

BOJ's Tankan: released quarterly, around the end of the current quarter.

AUSTRALIA

Unemployment Change: change in the number of employed people during the previous month. Job creation is an important leading indicator of consumer spending, which accounts for a majority of overall economic activity. Released monthly, about 15 days after the month ends.

Unemployment Rate: percentage of the total workforce that is unemployed and actively seeking employment during the previous month. Released monthly, about 15 days after the month ends.

GDP: change in the inflation-adjusted value of all goods and services produced by the economy. Released quarterly, about 65 days after the quarter ends.

CPI q/q: change in the price of goods and services purchased by consumers. Released quarterly, about 25 days after the quarter ends.

Retail Sales m/m: change in the total value of sales at the retail level. Released monthly, about 35 days after the month ends.

Building Approvals: change in the number of new building approvals issued. It is an excellent gauge of future construction activity because obtaining government approval is among the first steps in constructing a new building. Construction is important because it produces a wide-reaching ripple effect, for example, jobs are created for the construction workers, subcontractors and inspectors are hired, and various services are purchased by the builder. Released monthly, about 30 days after the month ends.

Trade Balance: difference in value between imported and exported goods during the reported month. Export demand and currency demand are directly linked because foreigners must buy domestic currency to pay for the nation's exports. Export demand also impacts production and prices at domestic manufacturers. A positive number indicates that more goods were exported than imported. Released monthly, about 35 days after the month ends.

NEW ZEALAND

Unemployment Rate: percentage of the total workforce that is unemployed and actively seeking employment during the previous quarter. Released quarterly, about 35 days after the quarter ends.

GDP q/q: change in the inflation-adjusted value of all goods and services produced by the economy. Released quarterly, about 80 days after the quarter ends.

CPI q/q: change in the price of goods and services purchased by consumers. Released quarterly, about 18 days after the quarter ends.

PPI q/q: change in the price of goods and raw materials purchased by manufacturers. Released quarterly, about 50 days after the quarter ends.

Retail Sales: change in the total value of inflation-adjusted sales at the retail level. Released Quarterly, about 45 days after the quarter ends.

CHINA

GDP q/y: change in the inflation-adjusted value of all goods and services produced by the economy. It is the broadest measure of economic activity and the primary gauge of the economy's health. Data represents the quarterly value compared to the same quarter a year earlier. Chinese data can have a broad impact on the currency markets due to China's influence on the global economy and investor sentiment. Released quarterly, about 18 days after the quarter ends.

Unemployment Rate: percentage of the total urban workforce that is unemployed and actively seeking employment during the previous month. Although it is generally viewed as a lagging indicator, the number of unemployed people is an important signal of overall economic health because consumer spending is highly correlated with labour-market conditions. Unemployment is also a major consideration for those steering the country's monetary policy. Released monthly, excluding February, about 15 days after the month ends.

Industrial Production: change in the total inflation-adjusted value of output produced by manufacturers, mines, and utilities. It is a leading indicator of economic health - production is the dominant driver of the economy and reacts quickly to ups and downs in the business cycle. Chinese data can have a broad impact on the currency markets due to China's influence on the global economy and investor sentiment. Released monthly, excluding Feb, about 15 days after the month ends.

Manufacturing PMI: level of a diffusion index based on surveyed purchasing managers in the manufacturing industry. Survey of 3,000 purchasing managers which asks respondents to rate the relative level of business conditions including employment, production, new orders, prices, supplier deliveries, and inventories.

It is a leading indicator of economic health-businesses react quickly to market conditions, and their purchasing managers hold perhaps the most current and relevant insight into the company's view of the economy.

It tends to have more impact when it is released ahead of the Caixin Manufacturing PMI because the reports are tightly correlated. Chinese data can have a broad impact on the currency markets due to China's influence on the global economy and investor sentiment. Released monthly, on the last day of the current month.

Caixin Service PMI: level of a diffusion index based on surveyed purchasing managers in the services industry. Survey of about 400 purchasing managers which asks respondents to rate the relative level of business conditions including employment, production, new orders, prices, supplier deliveries, and inventories.

It is a leading indicator of economic health-businesses react quickly to market conditions, and their purchasing managers hold perhaps the most current and relevant insight into the company's view of the economy. Released monthly, on the third business day after the month ends.

CPI y/y: change in the price of goods and services purchased by consumers. Consumer prices account for a majority of overall inflation. Inflation is important to currency valuation because rising prices lead the central bank to respond by raising interest rates. The average price of various goods and services are sampled and then compared to the sampling done a year earlier. Released monthly, usually about 10 days after the month ends.

PPI y/y: change in the price of goods purchased and sold by producers. It is a leading indicator of consumer inflation when producers pay and charge more for goods the higher costs are usually passed on to the consumer. Released monthly, usually about 10 days after the month ends.

Trade Balance: the difference in value between imported and exported goods during the previous month. Export demand and currency demand are directly linked because foreigners usually buy domestic currency to pay for the nation's exports. Export demand also impacts production and prices of domestic manufacturers. Released monthly, about 10 days after the month ends.

ECONOMIC PROJECTIONS

CHAPTER 8

In the Economic projections, there are the basic points of the American economy, which are revised every three months. It is very important because it gives us a clearer vision of the forecast and, therefore, of what the market expects. If these expectations are not met, the market will tend to react negatively, and that will weaken the USD.

Let's see the table of the Economic Projections released on December 14, 2016 (figure 4).

What can we deduce from it? Here we see described the **GDP** expected in 2016, 2017, 2018 and 2019, and as it was the past projection (September). As we can see, the GDP was revised slightly upwards except for 2018 (unchanged). What does this mean? That the Fed expects an acceleration of the US economy in the future.

That was also one of the springs that pushed Eur-Usd downward in January before other dynamics replaced it. Why? Because a future target had been revised upwards, thus the market was satisfied; therefore, the US Dollar was bought and consequently the EUR-USD fell.

Economic projections of Federal Reserve Board members and Federal Reserve Bank presidents under their individual assessments of projected appropriate monetary policy, December 2016
Advance release of table 1 of the Summary of Economic Projections to be released with the FOMC minutes

Percent

Variable	Median[1]					Central tendency[2]					Range[3]				
	2016	2017	2018	2019	Longer run	2016	2017	2018	2019	Longer run	2016	2017	2018	2019	Longer run
Change in real GDP	1.9	2.1	2.0	1.9	1.8	1.8 – 1.9	1.9 – 2.3	1.8 – 2.2	1.8 – 2.0	1.8 – 2.0	1.8 – 2.0	1.7 – 2.4	1.7 – 2.3	1.5 – 2.2	1.6 – 2.2
September projection	1.8	2.0	2.0	1.8	1.8	1.7 – 1.9	1.9 – 2.2	1.8 – 2.1	1.7 – 2.0	1.7 – 2.0	1.7 – 2.0	1.6 – 2.5	1.5 – 2.3	1.6 – 2.2	1.6 – 2.2
Unemployment rate	4.7	4.5	4.5	4.5	4.8	4.7 – 4.8	4.5 – 4.6	4.3 – 4.7	4.3 – 4.8	4.7 – 5.0	4.7 – 4.8	4.4 – 4.7	4.2 – 4.7	4.1 – 4.8	4.5 – 5.0
September projection	4.8	4.6	4.5	4.6	4.8	4.7 – 4.9	4.5 – 4.7	4.4 – 4.7	4.4 – 4.8	4.7 – 5.0	4.7 – 4.9	4.4 – 4.8	4.3 – 4.9	4.2 – 5.0	4.5 – 5.0
PCE inflation	1.5	1.9	2.0	2.0	2.0	1.5	1.7 – 2.0	1.9 – 2.0	2.0 – 2.1	2.0	1.5 – 1.6	1.7 – 2.0	1.8 – 2.2	1.8 – 2.2	2.0
September projection	1.3	1.9	2.0	2.0	2.0	1.2 – 1.4	1.7 – 1.9	1.8 – 2.0	1.9 – 2.0	2.0	1.1 – 1.7	1.5 – 2.0	1.8 – 2.0	1.8 – 2.1	2.0
Core PCE inflation[4]	1.7	1.8	2.0	2.0		1.7 – 1.8	1.8 – 1.9	1.9 – 2.0	2.0		1.6 – 1.8	1.7 – 2.0	1.8 – 2.2	1.8 – 2.2	
September projection	1.7	1.8	2.0	2.0		1.6 – 1.8	1.7 – 1.9	1.9 – 2.0	2.0		1.5 – 2.0	1.6 – 2.0	1.8 – 2.0	1.8 – 2.1	
Memo: Projected appropriate policy path															
Federal funds rate	0.6	1.4	2.1	2.9	3.0	0.6	1.1 – 1.6	1.9 – 2.6	2.4 – 3.3	2.8 – 3.0	0.6	0.9 – 2.1	0.9 – 3.4	0.9 – 3.9	2.5 – 3.8
September projection	0.6	1.1	1.9	2.6	2.9	0.6 – 0.9	1.1 – 1.8	1.9 – 2.8	2.4 – 3.0	2.8 – 3.0	0.4 – 1.1	0.6 – 2.1	0.6 – 3.1	0.6 – 3.8	2.5 – 3.8

NOTE: Projections of change in real gross domestic product (GDP) and projections for both measures of inflation are percent changes from the fourth quarter of the previous year to the fourth quarter of the year indicated. PCE inflation and core PCE inflation are the percentage rates of change in, respectively, the price index for personal consumption expenditures (PCE) and the price index for PCE excluding food and energy. Projections for the unemployment rate are for the average civilian unemployment rate in the fourth quarter of the year indicated. Each participant's projections are based on his or her assessment of appropriate monetary policy. Longer-run projections represent each participant's assessment of the rate to which each variable would be expected to converge under appropriate monetary policy and in the absence of further shocks to the economy. The projections for the federal funds rate are the value of the midpoint of the projected appropriate target range for the federal funds rate or the projected appropriate target level for the federal funds rate at the end of the specified calendar year or over the longer run. The September projections were made in conjunction with the meeting of the Federal Open Market Committee on September 20–21, 2016. One participant did not submit longer-run projections for the change in real GDP, the unemployment rate, or the federal funds rate in conjunction with the September 20–21, 2016, meeting, and one participant did not submit such projections in conjunction with the December 13–14, 2016, meeting.
  1. For each period, the median is the middle projection when the projections are arranged from lowest to highest. When the number of projections is even, the median is the average of the two middle projections.
  2. The central tendency excludes the three highest and three lowest projections for each variable in each year.
  3. The range for a variable in a given year includes all participants' projections, from lowest to highest, for that variable in that year.
  4. Longer-run projections for core PCE inflation are not collected.

Figure 4 - Economic Projections December 2016

The next entry is the **Unemployment Rate** and here, except for 2018 that remained unchanged, for all other years the rate was revised downwards from the September projection.

As regards data on employment, I digress lightly. The "quality" of wages (Average Hourly Earnings) holds much importance. What do I mean with "quality?" If wages do not increase, neither does the quality of work, and therefore, inflation will not rise. The number of employees can grow, but if they do not increase their purchasing power (their wages), we make little progress. That is one of the key points, and I always invite you to keep it in strong consideration in your analysis.

Moving on, we have **PCE inflation** which has seen, for the year 2016, a rise in the September forecast from 1.3 to 1.5 and this was the second important cause that has led to a strengthening of the US Dollar.

The increase in inflation relative to 2016 is a consequence of the appreciation of different commodities, especially crude oil.

The next entry is the **Core PCE Inflation**, and this is inflation without the energy component and, in fact, for the speech just made, remained unchanged both for 2016 and for all subsequent years. That is because, by excluding the energy, the other factors are easier to control.

The last point that we must consider and which helped the markets in their bullish trends is the prospect of increased interest rates. We can see this entry under **Federal Funds Rate** and if the rate was previously planned for 2017 to 1.1 now is expected to 1.4. That means that in 2017, there will be three rate hikes in the United States. Forecast revised upwards, consequently, also for the next two years.

This programmatic table is reviewed every three months (March, June, September and December), and on these occasions, there is always a little more attention, more volatility. So, these meetings are much more important than intermediate. The interest rates are much more likely to be raised or cut in one of these four months than those intermediates.

It is essential to understand the expectations of the American economy because the more we know, the more we can understand where the global market can move. Since it will surely have a significant impact on the Dollar, but also on all financial markets - since they are all a chain - it is therefore very important to know all its aspects in as detailed a manner as possible.

And finally, the table shows, in the top, three items: Median, Central Tendency, and Range. Below the table, there is the explanation of their meaning. However, we do not complicate our life too much. We look only to the Median because that is where we have to focus. If we want to do a study, as mentioned, below the table there are all the explanations - but let us not complicate matters. We have plenty of information as it is - focus on the Median data.

In the next chapter, we are going to see some of the most important macroeconomic data, the kind of data that moves markets as well as currencies.

NON-FARM PAYROLLS

CHAPTER 9

As introduced, the **Non-Farm Payrolls** is the data that moves both markets and currencies. Usually, it is released on the first Friday of the month together with two other major data regarding employment: the **Unemployment Rate** and **Average Hourly Earnings**.

It is essential to read the various industries that make up the report and evaluate them on the whole. A data could be lower than expected, but if in any industry has been increasing employment, the data is equally positive.

We can see an example of Non-Farm Payrolls in figure 5. This table always has the same structure; therefore, it will always be identical every time. Usually, we can find the table on page 5 or 6 of the report, and it is normally called "Employment by Selected Industry."

What we find here is the employment for each industry and, in the last entry, the Government.

ESTABLISHMENT DATA
Summary table B. Establishment data, seasonally adjusted

Category	Feb. 2016	Dec. 2016	Jan. 2017p	Feb. 2017p
EMPLOYMENT BY SELECTED INDUSTRY (Over-the-month change, in thousands)				
Total nonfarm	237	155	238	235
Total private	221	150	221	227
Goods-producing	-7	32	54	95
Mining and logging	-18	2	3	9
Construction	23	12	40	58
Manufacturing	-12	18	11	28
Durable goods[1]	-13	13	7	10
Motor vehicles and parts	1.2	0.9	2.7	-3.5
Nondurable goods	1	5	4	18
Private service-providing	228	118	167	132
Wholesale trade	-1.5	1.8	5.9	9.9
Retail trade	48.4	13.3	39.9	-26.0
Transportation and warehousing	3.2	13.4	-10.2	8.8
Utilities	0.7	0.2	-0.4	-1.0
Information	10	-6	-3	0
Financial activities	6	22	32	7
Professional and business services[1]	25	36	46	37
Temporary help services	-6.7	-17.4	6.5	3.1
Education and health services[1]	74	50	21	62
Health care and social assistance	52.0	39.2	26.1	32.5
Leisure and hospitality	45	5	24	26
Other services	17	-17	12	8
Government	16	5	17	8
(3-month average change, in thousands)				
Total nonfarm	201	148	186	209
Total private	183	153	183	199
WOMEN AND PRODUCTION AND NONSUPERVISORY EMPLOYEES AS A PERCENT OF ALL EMPLOYEES[2]				
Total nonfarm women employees	49.5	49.6	49.6	49.6
Total private women employees	48.0	48.2	48.1	48.2
Total private production and nonsupervisory employees	82.4	82.4	82.5	82.5
HOURS AND EARNINGS ALL EMPLOYEES Total private				
Average weekly hours	34.5	34.4	34.4	34.4
Average hourly earnings	$25.38	$25.98	$26.03	$26.09
Average weekly earnings	$875.61	$893.71	$895.43	$897.50
Index of aggregate weekly hours (2007=100)[3]	105.1	106.2	106.4	106.6
Over-the-month percent change	-0.1	0.4	0.2	0.2
Index of aggregate weekly payrolls (2007=100)[4]	127.5	131.9	132.4	133.0
Over-the-month percent change	0.0	0.7	0.4	0.5
DIFFUSION INDEX (Over 1-month span)[5]				
Total private (261 industries)	58.6	60.0	58.0	63.0
Manufacturing (78 industries)	48.1	53.8	50.0	65.4

[1] Includes other industries, not shown separately.

[2] Data relate to production employees in mining and logging and manufacturing, construction employees in construction, and nonsupervisory employees in the service-providing industries.

[3] The indexes of aggregate weekly hours are calculated by dividing the current month's estimates of aggregate hours by the corresponding annual average aggregate hours.

[4] The indexes of aggregate weekly payrolls are calculated by dividing the current month's estimates of aggregate weekly payrolls by the corresponding annual average aggregate weekly payrolls.

[5] Figures are the percent of industries with employment increasing plus one-half of the industries with unchanged employment, where 50 percent indicates an equal balance between industries with increasing and decreasing employment.

p Preliminary

NOTE: Data have been revised to reflect March 2016 benchmark levels and updated seasonal adjustment factors.

Figure 5 - Non-Farm Payrolls February 2017

The last two columns are the ones that we have to focus our attention on, in this case, January 2017 and February 2017. What we need to do is very visual work. It will help us not only to work with the data but also to get a view of the industries which may be more active or have more problems. And this can be useful, for example, if we need to make a selection of equity securities of a specific industry.

The first thing we need to do is to start the analysis with the "Mining and logging"; this is the hardest industry of all.

The data, as we can see, is showing clear signs of improvement and the industry is producing new employment. This data also tells us: if we are thinking of investing in securities (or options) in mining, they may have a good price increase, thanks to an improvement in employment and thus to the expansion of the industry.

It should be noted that a lot of this increase in employment is due to oil prices, in relation to the extractions that are made. The crude oil price from November to early March 2016 grew more than 20%; consequently, the workers have also increased.

Below "Mining and logging", we can find all the other industries, and although the data was less than that of the previous month, there was no loss of employments or crises, but only a moment of transition. Even the "Retail trade" that has seen a decline in employment of 23K, is coming from a large increase in January of nearly 40K. With experience you will come to see that retail trade is the only industry that does important excursions.

If there were growing industries and others in crisis, then it would have sounded an alarm bell. I would have said: here there is something wrong. Instead, the data is more or less in line with the previous ones.

To have a complete overview of the data without doing all the reasoning made above (although I always recommend doing your own evaluations), we can visit the "Bureau of Labour" website and read the release on the data. Especially the three-four lines (but my advice is to read subsequent as well) after "Establishment Survey Data" which I reproduce below:

"Total Non-Farm Payrolls employment increased by 235,000 in February. Job gains occurred in construction, private educational services, manufacturing, health care and mining."

Here we have a reading of the data. However, I prefer to see the Non-Farm Payrolls split up into the different industries because, in this way, I have a broader and more complete view.

With a correct reading of the Non-Farm Payrolls, once it has reached the end of the period of euphoria subsequent at the exit of the data, we can professionally open a trade. We have to do what the investment banks do, but we will also have on our side the correct reading of the data.

In conclusion, when the data of the Non-Farm Payrolls comes out, the first movement is emotional, depending on the data value. We have to do an accurate reading of the data, industries, and quality of wages (Average Hourly Earnings) and this is the reason why, often, we can assist a reversal of Eur-Usd (as well as other currency pairs).

CORRELATION IN FOREX

CHAPTER 10

Let's see now another concept: correlation. **Correlation** is defined as the ratio of price developments of two markets. We will talk of correlated markets when to the increase of the first market we have an increase in the other and vice versa, so that most of the time, a descent of the first market corresponds with a decline in the second one.

The correlation coefficient is a measure that determines the degree to which two markets' movements are associated. The range of values for the correlation coefficient is -1.0 to 1.0. If a calculated correlation is greater than 1.0 or less than -1.0, a mistake has been made.

A correlation of 1.0 indicates a perfect positive correlation, while a correlation of -1.0 indicates a perfect negative correlation. 0.0 means that the two markets have no correlation; they are independent of each other.

When we speak of correlation between currencies, we refer to the movement of two currency pairs, which can be the same, opposite or random, according to a certain period of time. Since currencies are always exchanged in pairs, it is not possible for a currency to move as just one.

Are the correlations important? It depends, in Forex no. Indeed, correlations are very often harmful, and I will explain the reasons why. First of all, the correlations come and go.

It means that today two currency pairs can be correlated, but tomorrow they may not be. Looking at the correlations between different time-frames, we sometimes see very different values, precisely because they are not stable.

Therefore, setting a strategy based on the degree of correlation between the different currency pairs, it is likely that suddenly that correlation ceases; and the worst thing is that we will realise it only when we are getting a loss, without having the opportunity to modify the trade first.

"If Eur-Usd rises, then Gbp-Usd will rise as well." Probable but it is not certain because when we create a currency pair, we do nothing but oppose two economies, and the Eurozone economy is very different from the English one. Already it is not easy to evaluate two economies well; if then whilst chasing a correlation we add a third economy, our analysis becomes a lot more complicated.

A statement like "if we know the correlations, we can cover ourselves in case of loss" is totally wrong. The most stupid thing to do if we are long on Eur-Usd is to cover ourselves by selling Usd-Chf. We might as well close the position because in the positive case, the loss is kept steady, in the negative one, it increases because the correlation does not work.

The best thing to do if we want to protect our portfolio is to use safe-haven currencies, which we will encounter in one of the following chapters.

The same goes for the diversification of the portfolio. "Instead of investing $ 20,000 on a long trade on Aud-Usd, we can invest $ 10,000 on the long of Aud-Usd and $ 10,000 on the long of Nzd-Usd." However, the above is not always a good strategy. The Australian and New Zealand economies are similar but different in some respects, such as, for example, the monetary policy. There are better ways to diversify a Forex portfolio.

The essential correlations that every Forex trader must know are those between currencies and commodities. Some economies are mainly based on the export of commodities. The currencies of these countries are called Commodity Currencies. The currencies most traded that belong to this category are CAD (Canadian Dollar), AUD (Australian Dollar), and NZD (New Zealand Dollar).

I complete the chapter by saying that I do not use correlations between currencies in my trading, but everyone is free to think differently. For those interested, in the Myfxbook website (https://www.myfxbook.com/forex-market/correlation), you can find the correlation table. You can select the time-frame and currency pairs of your interest.

You can verify yourself that passing from 1 day to 1 week and to 1 month the correlation values change, a lot sometimes. The same is the case for smaller time-frames.

THE OPERATIONAL PLAN

CHAPTER 11

This scenario that we have created becomes a starting point not only for the analysis of currencies but is also a fundamental step for balancing and consolidation of our portfolio. Our goal is to buy currencies with the greatest strengths and to sell the ones that are subject to adverse scenarios.

Important. This is a basic concept, and I have already repeated it. It is the cornerstone of the entire analysis, which otherwise would not make sense. All our work is focused on analysing the two economies (the two currencies that make up the currency pair) to establish with certainty which of the two is the strongest, and therefore, what will be the future movement of the currency pair (always up to when the initial conditions will not change).

So, how to operationalise the scenario that we have built? firstly, every system follows some key points and levels that we have to define at the start. Then, all we have to do is draw in the chart sensitive levels where news, reports and speeches have created movements or the price will tend to move in a particular way.

I am talking about supports and resistances, both technical and fundamental, and that we will see better in the following two chapters. As said, supports and resistances are the only aspect of technical analysis I use in my analysis.

I like to set up wide-ranging operations, that is, I like to make sure that I can manage the operation so that even though there is a movement against my position, this does not put me in trouble. So, first I insert a first order for testing the market, a "spy-order", usually of a small amount, of course, always proportionate to the whole position. Personally, for the spy-order, I use 1/4 of the entire position (however, never more than 1/3).

Then, I insert a higher primary-order concerning the size, just to rebalance the average price and be able to better ride the operation (obviously, the whole order has to respect my position sizing).

Why more than one market entry? Because by doing only one market entry with the whole position, we risk inserting a stop-loss much narrower, which would mean that managing the position would become much more inconvenient than just splitting the market entry with a first spy-order, followed by a primary-order.

The size of the spy-order, however, should not be too small since it must also be fruitful in case the price does not reach the level of the primary-order. We have to be proportionate in what we do. The spy-order cannot be too small or large because the optic of the operation is wide-ranging.

In addition to the market entry, we also have to establish stop-loss and target profit levels. The stop-loss is mainly mathematical because the first thing we have to look for is our equity. We are not going to invest a percentage that overcomes our risk management. So, we insert the stop-loss based on what we want to risk, a stop-loss on the equity.

While the stop-loss level is fixed and irremovable (to that level we have to close the trade), about the target, I like to see how the currency pair comes to that price, and if there is space for making the operation run a little (or whether it is wiser to close it down early). That is the reason why I do not want to give any rules, because the markets are not the same every day, and the scenarios can change at any time.

Conversely, a stop-loss must never be modified, or rather, if we move it to reduce risk, it is always positive, but once we decided an exit level, we must respect it. This is also because, by working with a stop-loss on the equity, moving the stop means increasing the loss that we had decided in our trading plan, and this does not make us feel more comfortable with that trade.

How do we decide where to put the primary-order? Once the spy-order is executed, what are the possible scenarios? Let me give an example: we sell Eur-Usd. If the currency pair falls, it goes to our advantage, meaning the spy-order will gain us a profit. If the market rises, then we will choose an excess level, where to open the primary-order. An excess level, that is, above a "fundamental resistance" created by a decision of a central bank.

Here, we are faced with another concept inherent in investment banks, the subjective probability, that is, the numeric measure of chance (probability) that reflects the degree of a personal belief in the likelihood of an occurrence.

In my two years as a fund manager, I changed my mentality and understood the importance of subjective probability for market entry (contrary to what you can read on the internet). I have dedicated one of the next chapters to this argument.

In conclusion, you have to work on the excesses. Never be satisfied with the current price, but always aim, thanks to the sensitive levels, to work on the price excesses in order to reap additional benefits from the market.

Technical Support/Resistance

CHAPTER 12

As I said, I do not use technical analysis; the subjective probability (you will see this better later on) gives me the entry points. However, beginners can initially get help by drawing static supports and resistances on the chart.

The key is the existing monetary policy difference between two economies that suggests which currency pairs offer the most excellent opportunities for trading, at any given time. The goal of every trader is to evaluate daily market conditions and, eventually, modify the strategy accordingly if and when something changes.

The first step is the study of macroeconomics on a global scale. We have to establish the backdrop at the highest level to be able to filter the data and reach the dynamics of currency pairs at the lowest level.

In doing so, we will examine the monetary policies of major central banks and a few other indicators (the most important). In this phase, it is very important that the trader takes into account only the data, without giving importance to the rumours.

So, what we have to do is understand the different monetary policies of central banks and analyse the economic developments of a country through the macroeconomic data.

However, this is not enough because once we have done a comprehensive analysis of two economies, this gives us an insight of which economy (and therefore currency) is stronger, but it does not give us a level for market entry (timing).

If, for example, we have established that the Canadian economy is expanding, while New Zealand is in a contraction phase, it does not mean that Nzd-Cad will fall tomorrow.

What we have to do is search for a good level to open a bearish position on the currency pair. What I do is search on the chart for a resistance where Nzd-Cad is not "insensitive", an instance that represents an excellent market entry (even though there are other considerations to make).

Before moving on to some practical examples, we have to see various types of supports and resistances. Let's look at the definitions again.

A level is defined as **"support"** when the demand is particularly strong, and sellers cannot overwhelm it. A support level is all the more significant if in the past it has been tested multiple times without breaking.

So, the support reflects the inability of a market to drop below a certain price level. Below, we can see an example of support with the Eur-Gbp daily chart (figure 6).

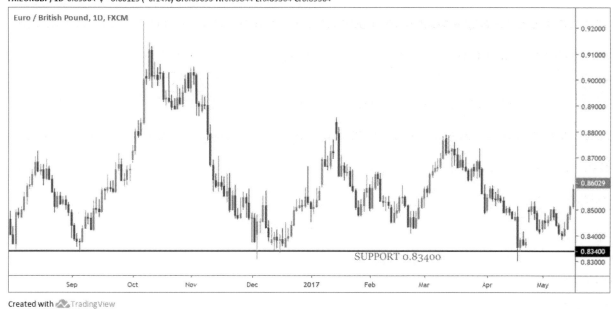

Figure 6 - Eur-Gbp daily chart with support (TradingView.com)

Figure 7 - Aud-Cad daily chart with resistance (TradingView.com)

A level is defined as "**resistance**" when the offer is particularly strong, and buyers cannot win against sellers. A resistance level becomes more significant the more times it has been tested without breaking.

So, the resistance reflects the inability of a market to climb above a certain price level. Above, we can see an example of resistance with the Aud-Cad daily chart (figure 7).

Figure 8 - Nzd-Jpy weekly chart change of polarity (TradingView.com)

There are two types of support/resistance: static and dynamic.

- A "**static**" support/resistance level corresponds to a precise and constant point in time, such as the high and low of the year, or a Fibonacci retracement (we will come across these in a minute).

- A **"dynamic"** support/resistance level, instead, changes its value as time passes.

Supports and resistances over time tend to be overcome, in such cases, an old resistance becomes new support, and past support turns into new resistance. There is a ***change of polarity***, as shown above in the Nzd-Jpy weekly chart (figure 8).

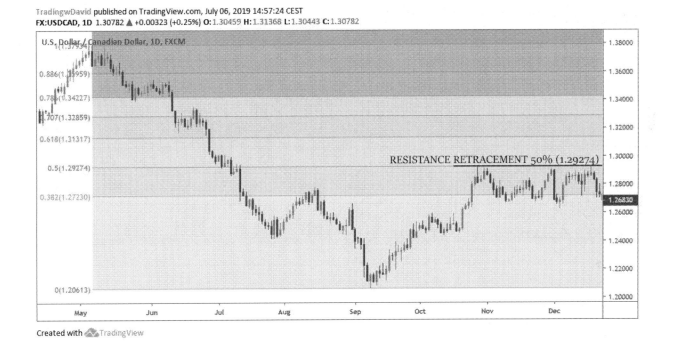

Figure 9 - Usd-Cad daily chart with Fibonacci (TradingView.com)

Fibonacci retracements give the second type of static support and resistance.

Fibonacci retracements consist of horizontal intervals that correspond to Fibonacci levels such as 23.6%, 38.2%, 50%, and 61.8%.

The Fibonacci retracements can be considered supports and resistances, as shown above in the Usd-Cad daily chart (figure 9). Observe how the price meets resistance on 50% Fibonacci retracement. If we look at the downtrend of Usd-Cad, we can easily see that every time the currency pair rebounds, the retracement ends at a Fibonacci level (23.8% or 38%).

It will not always be so, especially because we do not know where a currency pair will stop the rebound (38.2% 50% or maybe 61.8). But that is common for all the static resistances (and supports).

Another type of static support and resistance is given by the **highs and lows of the previous years**. Often, they are significant levels where the market is not insensitive as shown in figure 10 with the chart of Aud-Usd.

Figure 10 - Aud-Usd daily chart (TradingView.com)

In particular, for those of you who are beginner, to draw the lows and highs of previous years in the chart can be an excellent way to find important levels that the market will find hard to overcome.

The **gaps**, the Windows in the candlestick analysis, are another static level that often sees the formation of supports and resistances. The gaps in forex are sporadic and can occur only between the close of Friday and the open of Sunday.

Very often, moreover, the gaps hide the willingness of the currency pair to go in the opposite direction as the chart of Gbp-Cad in figure 11 shows where, after the gap down, the currency pair has risen by about 900 pips in a few days.

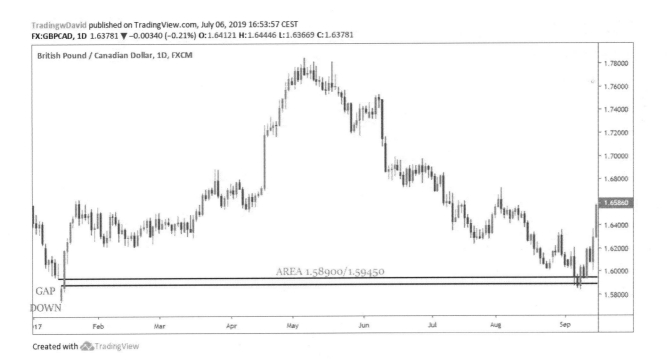

Figure 11 - Gbp-Cad daily chart (TradingView.com)

Now, let's see the dynamic support and resistance. The most used is the trendline. A line that follows the lows (support) or the highs (resistance) of a trend, as we can see in figure 12 with the Eur-Chf daily chart.

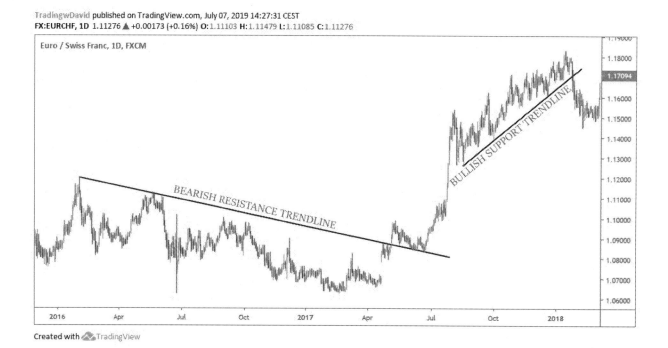

Figure 12 - Eur-Chf daily chart (TradingView.com)

The second commonly used way of finding dynamic supports and resistances is the moving average.

A **moving average** is an indicator used by traders, and that is based on historical price trends. A moving average is calculated on a certain quantity of price data (period) and is "moving" because it moves from day to day (or other time-frame) precisely because of its calculation method.

So, by way of example, if we want to calculate a 20-day moving average of the Eur-Usd price, to update it, it will be enough to add to the series the data of today's close, eliminating the close price of 20 days ago.

In practical terms, a 20-day moving average represents the average value of the last 20 trading sessions, and each data will weight 1/20 of the series. The longer the period we are considering, the less the data that we gradually add will affect the moving average. Thus, a 20-day moving average will be less affected by new data than a 5-day moving average, and more than a 100-day moving average.

Figure 13 below shows the Aud-Nzd chart to which has been applied the 200-day simple moving average.

Figure 13 - Aud-Nzd daily chart with 200-day moving average (TradingView.com)

Generally, the 200-day moving average is used as a watershed between bullish and bearish trends. If a currency pair is above the moving average, it is in an uptrend, if it is below, it is a bearish trend.

Nowadays, all the trading platforms facilitate an easy insertion of graphic data which represents the moving average of a price. So, to visualise them on a chart, we no longer have to worry about using graph paper, pencil and calculator, as the chart analysis pioneers did.

Complementing this introduction on the moving average, I add that there are different kinds of them depending on the formula used.

The Simple Moving Average (SMA) is the classic one, and the one we have seen above. The Exponential Moving Average (EMA) and the Weighted Moving Average (WMA) are the others most utilised.

As said, in the **Simple Moving Average (SMA)**, each data will get the same weight in the series. If, for example, we use a 14-day SMA, each data will weight 1/14 of the series.

The **Exponential Moving Average (EMA)**, instead, gives more weight to the most recent data. This kind of moving average reacts faster to recent price changes than a simple moving average.

Finally, the **Weighted Moving Average (WMA)**. It gives more weight on recent data and less on past ones (similarly to the Exponential Moving Average). This is done by multiplying every single price by a weighting factor. Because of its unique calculation, WMA will follow prices more closely than a corresponding

Simple Moving Average.

Other often-used periods are 21, 34 and 55. We can see an example in figure 14 with the Aud-Usd daily chart with applied the 55-day Exponential Moving Average.

Figure 14 - Aud-Usd daily chart with 55-day EMA (TradingView.com)

However, the moving averages work well as dynamic supports and resistances as long as the currency pair is in trend. When, instead, the price moves sideways, they become "unusable."

We can see an example of that in the Eur-Jpy daily chart with the 21-day Simple Moving Average (figure 15).

Figure 15 - Eur-Jpy daily chart with 21-day SMA (TradingView.com)

In conclusion, static supports and resistances are not part of my subjective probability; however, they can help less-experienced traders to initially find some sensitive levels of a currency pair.

Once again, I do not take into account technical analysis. I do not consider any pattern or indicator when I work with currencies. If you desire to become a professional trader, you should do the same.

In the next chapter, we are going to see the fundamental supports and resistances, that is, the ones created by the decisions of the Central Banks.

FUNDAMENTAL SUPPORT/RESISTANCE

CHAPTER 13

When we analyse a currency pair, we usually see as united. Instead we need to see, and learn to work with them by separating the two currencies. As a result, we have to work with two individual economies.

Figure 16 - Aud-Usd daily chart (TradingView.com)

Now let's see a concrete example with Aud-Usd. First, I start analysing the Australian economy, and after I will do the same with the US one. My goal is to buy where there is strength and to sell where there is a weakness. Above in figure 16, we can see the Aud-Usd daily chart with two "fundamental" resistances.

On the chart, as I said, we can see highlighted two levels, the first at 0.77000 is that of the last cut in Australian interest rates on July 6, 2016. The lower level at 0.7500 is that of the last hike in interest rates in the US on December 14, 2017 (although the latter had already been priced into the market during the previous weeks).

We can see also a static resistance area at 0.77000/0.77500 that has worked perfectly in the past, and from there, Aud-Usd has always dropped at a lower price.

I analyse now, as mentioned, the two individual economies, starting with the **Australian** one.

PROS:

- Growth in GDP, it is expected to be 3% this year.

CONS:

- Exports-based economy. It depends on other economies (China) and the prices of commodities;
- End of the mining investment boom;
- Moderate consumptions;

- The continuing slowdown of growth in labour costs means that inflation is expected to remain low for some time;
- An appreciating exchange rate would complicate the growth.

We have already seen the **US economy** analysis in a previous chapter, but for convenience, I rewrite it below:

<u>PROS</u>:

- Domestic consumption-based economy;
- Currency used for international trade;
- Good data regarding employment;
- Economy growing at a faster rate;
- Three projected interest rate hikes in 2017.

<u>CONS</u>:

- Political uncertainty caused by Donald Trump;
- Problems with the budget deficit;
- USD too strong with penalisation for exports.

From the analysis made, it is clear that the US economy is stronger than that of Australia, and if there are no changes, the US currency will appreciate in the medium-term more than the Australian one. So, area 0.77000 is a reasonable level when selling Aud-Usd, particularly because there is an excess of price.

Aud-Usd, like all the currency pairs, has its characteristics. When in the chart there are candles with very long shadows (and very tight bodies), it means that the currency pair is in a decision-making phase. The explosion may be very strong, given its nature. The relationship between the commodities (in particular gold and silver) and AUD is very special (we will see this in a later chapter).

Correlations such as Aud-Usd and gold remain standing on equal terms, but when the variables are moved, like with the interest rates, correlations no longer exist, and any other variable should not be regarded because the Central Bank decision changes the cards on the table. So, correlation works until things remain the same. When the parameters change, the interest rates, in this case, have the advantage of everything else.

Looking at the interest rates, as well as what the central bank does and says is key, since it is the central banks that mostly drive the currency pairs. If they do nothing, we can take the field with all the relationships that we have. So, exports, commodities, everything. But if interest rates move, there is nothing else that matters.

A rate hike is a sign of the strength of the currency (and economy). Rising interest rate is needed to put a stop to inflation. Inflation is generated when the economy proceeds at a fast pace, and it means that companies have produced, and continue to produce a lot. There is health in the labour-market. So, all of this translates into a great strength for that currency.

So, what we have to consider are interest rates when we work with Forex and the currencies; they are what establishes the cost of money. However, when the rates remain unchanged, especially for a long time, the market finds other correlations. However, when rates remain unchanged, especially for a long time, the market finds other correlations. In the case of Aud-Usd, these correlations are to do with gold, oil and China, due to exportations from Australia.

Concerning the macroeconomic levels (fundamental supports and resistances), more volatile currency pairs sometimes tend to overtake them. They tend to respect them later, in the medium to long-term.

However, some significant spikes can do it. Because they have less liquidity than the "Majors", and therefore, they are more subject to higher variations. And then, as already said, short-term speculation moves the markets.

Figure 17 - Nzd-Usd daily chart (TradingView.com)

Now, to complete this chapter, let's see a couple of other examples. In figure 17 above, we can see the Nzd-Usd daily chart, similar to what we saw with

Aud-Usd but a weaker New Zealand economy than the Australian one has led the currency pair to a deeper downward movement.

We find two levels highlighted in the chart. The most recent rate cut in New Zealand, and that of the last rate hike in the United States.

The second example concerns Usd-Cad. We can see the daily chart in figure 18.

Figure 18 - Usd-Cad daily chart (TradingView.com)

Here again, the two fundamental supports highlighted (the last rate cut in Canada and the most recent rate hike in the United States) have worked very well. That will not be forever since, sooner or later, the conditions will change, but until then, these macroeconomic levels will tend to be respected. And especially what I call "excesses of price" may provide us with excellent opportunities to trade.

SOME MONTHS LATER

CHAPTER 14

We saw fundamental support and resistance that form when central banks make monetary policy decisions. They are very important and tend to be respected. Although, from time to time we witness an excess in price that represents good levels that enable us to open positions.

Figure 19 - Eur-Usd weekly chart (TradingView.com)

This is for as long as conditions remain unchanged; when they do, fundamental support or resistance may also mean having no more value, which I will demonstrate with an example. Above we find the Eur-Usd daily chart already seen previously (figure 19).

Here is the same chart a few months later (figure 20).

Figure 20 - Eur-Usd weekly chart (TradingView.com)

The fundamental resistance that had been created by the introduction of Quantitative Easing by the ECB was wiped out. How is this possible? This is actually not that surprising. What has happened is that the initial conditions have been modified. On July 20th, at the ECB's meeting, chairman Mario Draghi, responding to a question, implied that the QE might have come to an end: *"in autumn, we should talk about changes to the ECB's stimulus policies."*

In the September 7 meeting, he confirmed that the QE, in its current form, is going to end on December 2017. Draghi also added that *"the increase in exchange rates is largely endogenous, caused by the strength of the European economy."* Between the lines, we can read that the Eurozone economy is starting to grow, and that the QE is no longer necessary.

Between the two meetings, on the 25th of August, there were the words, or better, what was not said, by the Fed chair Janet Yellen, who did not tackle a discussion on rates of interest, leaving us to infer that a third cut in 2017 is not that certain. So, as we can see, at the monetary policy level, there have been several changes, and these, coupled with the economic performance of the Euro area and of the United States (which we will see more clearly in the next chapter), contributed to the steep rise of Eur-Usd.

Figure 21 - Nzd-Usd daily chart (TradingView.com)

Even the charts seen in the previous chapter have had, at least initially, the same movement; although the motivations were different. Let's start by looking at the Nzd-Usd chart (figure 21 above).

The currency pair, from mid-May, began a strong bullish phase that led it to earn about 11%, reaching the resistance at 0.75200.

Then, it dropped from the area of the excess of the price, returning below the level of 0.73400, the fundamental resistance that has been created by the most recent cut in interest rates of the Reserve Bank of New Zealand.

Very similar to the movement that Aud-Usd made and that we can see in figure 22.

Figure 22 - Aud-Usd daily chart (TradingView.com)

The movement was the same, even though the drop of Aud-Usd was slightly less deep, due to the fact that the Australian economy is stronger than the New Zealand one.

Finally, in figure 23 we can see a Usd-Cad daily chart that, due to two interest rate rises decided by the Bank of Canada, has instead continued to fall.

Figure 23 - Usd-Cad daily chart (TradingView.com)

Only in recent weeks has the currency pair bounced, returning to test the fundamental resistance that has formed with the first rise in interest rates decided by the Canadian central bank.

So, what we have seen in this chapter is that the fundamental supports and resistances work very well until the conditions that led to their formation change.

Monetary policy decisions by central banks have led to the abolition of some key levels that had been formed over the last two years, together with the weakening or improvement of the economies of the individual countries.

We have also seen that there has been for NZD, AUD, and CAD a strong bullish movement against the US Dollar from mid-May to late July; then the three currency pairs have taken different directions. We will see the motives of these movements in the next chapter, and we will learn how to analyse a country's economy through its macroeconomic data.

MACRO-DATA ANALYSIS

CHAPTER 15

Now, we analyse the economies of the two countries that make up a currency pair, trying to evaluate their strengths in order to get an indication of the movements the currency pair could make in the coming months.

Let's begin with Eur-Usd (Table 1), first analysing the Eurozone and then the United States, which is done through the most important macroeconomic data that are released monthly or quarterly. It is very simple; we need to create tables with the main "indicators" that we will update after every release [Data 2017].

Macro-data	DEC	JAN	FEB	MAR	APR	MAY	JUN	JUL	AUG
Rate	0.0%	0.0%		0.0%	0.0%		0.0%	0.0%	
Unempl. Rate	9.8%	9.8%	9.6%	9.6%	9.5%	9.5%	9.3%	9.3%	9.1%
GDP			0.5%			0.5%			0.6%

Zew	13.8	16.6	10.4	12.8	19.5	20.6	18.6	17.5	10.0
Flash PMI	54.9	55.1	55.5	56.2	56.8	57.0	57.3	56.8	57.4
CPI y/y	1.1%	1.8%	2.0%	1.5%	1.9%	1.4%	1.3%	1.3%	1.5%
Retail Sales	1.1%	-0.4%	-0.3%	-0.1%	0.7%	0.3%	0.1%	0.4%	0.5%

Table 1 - Eurozone macroeconomic data (2017)

We have to do the same with the United States (Table 2).

Macro-data	DEC	JAN	FEB	MAR	APR	MAY	JUN	JUL	AUG
Rate	0.75		0.75	1.00		1.00	1.25	1.25	
NFP	178K	156K	227K	235K	98K	211K	138K	222K	209K
Av. Hr. Ern.	-0.1%	0.4%	0.1%	0.2%	0.2%	0.3%	0.2%	0.2%	0.3%
Unemp. Rate	4.6%	4.7%	4.8%	4.7%	4.5%	4.4%	4.3%	4.4%	4.3%
Adv. GDP		1.9%			0.7%			2.6%	
ISM Manuf.	53.2	54.7	56	57.7	57.2	54.8	54.9	57.8	56.3

CPI m/m	0.2%	0.3%	0.6%	0.1%	-0.3%	0.2%	-0.1%	0.0%	0.1%
PPI m/m	0.4%	0.3%	0.6%	0.3%	-0.1%	0.5%	0.0%	0.1%	-0.1%
Retail Sales	0.1%	0.6%	0.4%	0.1%	-0.2%	0.4%	-0.3%	-0.2%	0.6%
Building Perm	1.20M	1.21M	1.29M	1.21M	1.26M	1.23M	1.17M	1.25M	1.22M
Existing Home Sales	5.61M	5.49M	5.69M	5.48M	5.71M	5.57M	5.62M	5.52M	5.44M

Table 2 - United States macroeconomic data (2017)

For convenience, I have taken into account only data of the last nine months, but we can also take date from a longer period (it is advisable to have data for at least the previous 18/24 months for a good analysis).

At this point, we have to draw our conclusions. From the above data, the first thing we can deduce is that the American economy continues to grow moderately, with the gross domestic product expanded at a more sustained pace in the second quarter. Labour continues to strengthen with wages that growing not by much, but steadily every month. The unemployment rate has dropped by about half a percentage point since the beginning of the year.

Consumer price (CPI) is falling, which keeps inflation below 2% (Fed target) also because it is not helped by the energy component which, being crude oil, has been in a bearish trend for the last several months. Consumer spending data also declined slightly, although consumer confidence (data not shown) remained broadly unchanged.

Concerning the Eurozone, the data released confirmed Draghi's words on the growth of the Eurozone.

Gross domestic product (GDP) is expanding at a more sustained pace, increasing the final estimates for this year at 2.2%. Data regarding employment have improved, with the unemployment rate, which fell 0.8% in the first eight months of the year.

The Zew grows but remains below the long-term average of 23.8 points. Consumer prices (CPI) are on the rise, even though inflation remains below the 2% target (1.5% in August). Retail Sales data improves.

So, we have the US economy which is expanding at a moderate pace, while there are signs of major improvements in activity across the Eurozone.

Let's see other economies. We start with Australia, beginning always by building the table with the most important macroeconomic data (Table 3).

Macro-data	DEC	JAN	FEB	MAR	APR	MAY	JUN	JUL	AUG
Rate	1.50%		1.50%	1.50%	1.50%	1.50%	1.50%	1.50%	1.50%
Unemp. Change	39.1K	13.5K	13.5K	-6.4K	60.9K	37.4K	42.0K	14.0K	27.9K

Unemp. Rate	5.8%	5.7%	5.8%	5.9%	5.9%	5.7%	5.5%	5.6%	5.6%
GDP	-0.5%			1.1%			0.3%		
CPI q/q		0.5%			0.5%			0.2%	
Retail Sales	0.5%	0.2%	-0.1%	0.4%	-0.1%	-0.1%	1.0%	0.6%	0.3%
Build. Appr.	-12.6M	7.0M	-1.2M	1.8M	8.3M	-13.4M	4.4M	-5.6M	10.9M

Table 3 - Australia macroeconomic data (2017)

The Macroeconomic data draw a favourable situation for the Australian economy with the Gross Domestic Product expanding and expected at 3% in 2017, higher than initially estimated.

Inflation is also growing and is expected at 2% in the second half of the year. Falling unemployment rate in June has reached the lowest level since March 2013 (at 5.6% in August). Consumer spending data remains weak because of lower wage growth.

Increasing exports thanks not only to China, whose growth is higher than the estimates but also to the major advanced economies that have seen the growth in potential rates. Trade Balance (data not shown), in fact, after the last two years where only negative signs have been registered, this year has seen (at least so far) exports exceed imports.

The economy of Australia is, therefore, growing even higher than the estimates, and also the end of the mining boom now seems to be overcome. Only consumptions have not restarted vigorously.

Now, let's see the table with the macroeconomic data released by New Zealand (Table 4).

Macro-data	DEC	JAN	FEB	MAR	APR	MAY	JUN	JUL	AUG
Rate			1.75%	1.75%		1.75%	1.75%		1.75%
Unemp. Rate		5.2%				4.9%			4.8%
GDP	1.1%			0.4%			0.5%		
CPI q/q		0.4%			1.0%			0.0%	
PPI q/q			1.0%			0.8%			1.4%
Retail Sales		0.6%				1.5%			2.0%

Table 4 - New Zealand macroeconomic data (2017)

New Zealand has conflicting data. It grows the Gross Domestic Product, but by less than expected. Falling inflation because the oil and food price rises that had characterised 2017 are now missing, and (data not reported) the real

95

estate market has slowed.

Conversely, it raises consumer spending, due to strong population growth, and the employment with an unemployment rate dropped to 4.8%.

New Zealand after a stagnation period, which saw rates falling from 3.50% (April 29, 2015) to 1.75% (November 9, 2016), is trying to get out, and starting a growth phase, but it is still too weak.

Now the last analysis through the macroeconomic data. Let's see the Canadian economy (Table 5).

Macro-data	DEC	JAN	FEB	MAR	APR	MAY	JUN	JUL	AUG
Rate	0.5%	0.5%		0.5%	0.5%	0.5%		0.75%	
Unemp. Rate	6.8%	6.9%	6.8%	6.6%	6.7%	6.5%	6.6%	6.5%	6.3%
GDP m/m	-0.3%	0.4%	0.3%	0.6%	0.0%	0.5%	0.2%	0.6%	0.3%
CPI m/m	-0.4%	-0.2%	0.9%	0.2%	0.2%	0.4%	0.1%	-0.1%	0.0%
Manuf. Sales	-0.8%	1.5%	1.3%	0.6%	-0.2%	1.0%	1.1%	1.1%	-1.8%
Retail Sales	1.4%	0.1%	-0.3%	1.7%	-0.1%	-0.2%	1.5%	-0.1%	0.7%

Table 5 - Canada macroeconomic data (2017)

Canadian economic activity has grown strongly in recent quarters. Growth in GDP in the first quarter of 2017 has increased sharply to 3.7%. Inflation (CPI) is soft for the most part as a result of food, electricity and automobile prices. Consumer spending data is supported by the growing expansion of employment (unemployment rate in August touched the lowest since December 2008) and an increase in wage growth. Canada's exports have continued to recover and can be expected to keep expanding (data not shown).

Canada is in a phase of strong growth. Excluding inflation, still below the target of 2%, all other data shows a healthy economy far beyond expectations.

Now a clarification. The green, red and black colours of the various values in the tables (only in the pdf version) have a meaning. If a value compared to expectations was higher, the percentage/number is written in green, lower in red, and unchanged in black. In this way, we have, visually, a faster analysis. For example, we can quickly see that New Zealand's GDP is positive but less than expected.

In conclusion, we have seen that the USD bearish movement since mid-May is mainly due to a *"generalised US Dollar weakness as markets re-assess the likely pace of monetary policy normalisation in the United States."* That stands in opposition to a favourable economic situation, with the economies of major countries often growing beyond the estimates. However, depending on the currencies against which USD is opposed, the bearish movement has developed in different ways.

Nzd-Usd. After the peak on July 27, 2017, the currency pair has started to decline (also because the New Zealand economy is not yet in a well-established growth). From the excess of the price, the currency pair is back below the fundamental resistance in the 0.73400 area. The Governor of the Reserve Bank of New Zealand during the August meeting stressed that "*the exchange rate remains higher than is sustainable for balanced growth in the economy and continues to dampen import prices and tradables inflation.*"

Aud-Usd. Initially, the currency pair moved upwards on the highs thanks to the gold that pushed the Australian Dollar. International tensions (particularly with North Korea) helped the gold investment, which is, as we will see further on in this book, directly correlated to the Australian currency. Then, as it happened with Nzd-Usd, the currency pair started declining, and from the technical resistance, it went back to a correct price, below the fundamental resistance.

Usd-Cad. The currency pair has fallen sharply since May. A Canadian economy that grows at a faster pace than expected has led the Bank of Canada to raise rates twice (July 12 and September 9), and this has helped to push Usd-Cad even further down, reaching an area of 1.21000 (1700 pips lost in little more than four months).

So, from this analysis, we can comprehend why Aud-Usd remained near highs for a longer period of time, and why it later dropped less than Nzd-Usd (Australian economy stronger than the New Zealand one, and gold that rose from mid-July by about $ 150 an ounce).

Because Cad-Usd, despite crude oil was (and still is) anchored below $ 50 a barrel (we will see this better in the chapter on commodity currencies), it collapsed (the Canadian economy's strength and two rate hikes by the Bank of

Canada).

We have seen how to analyse the economy of a country through the macroeconomic data. At first glance, it may seem complicated, but with a little practice and experience, it will get easier to do. At this type of analysis, we must always add the statements and minutes of the central banks in order to get a complete picture of what market expectations are.

For example, if we look at the charts in the previous chapter, it becomes apparent that when US rates rose on March 15th and June 15th, at those times the US dollar had not strengthened, but actually weakened. The reason for the rate rises is mainly due to the high liquidity post QE. Expectations of the market were for something more, some more measures to absorb liquidity, that there have not been. Investors disappointed, Dollar sold.

In conclusion, I add that if we want to have a representation of the data with more visual impact, we can use graphs. Let's look at some examples, starting with the Canadian GDP in figure 24.

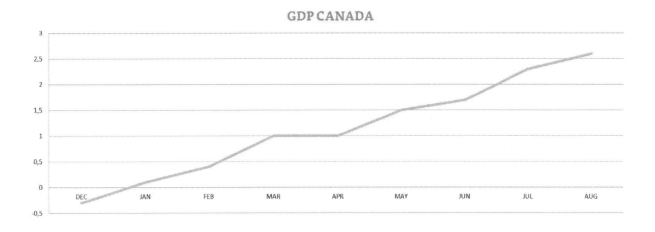

Figure 24 - GDP Canada

I added up the monthly data for a better reading. As we can see, in 9 months the Canadian GDP grew by 3%, going from -0.3% in December to 2.7% in August. Below are two other examples. In figure 25, the chart of the CPI of the United States and in figure 26, the Retail Sales of the Eurozone.

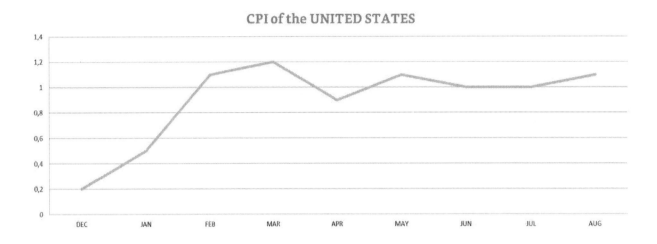

Figure 25 - CPI of the United States

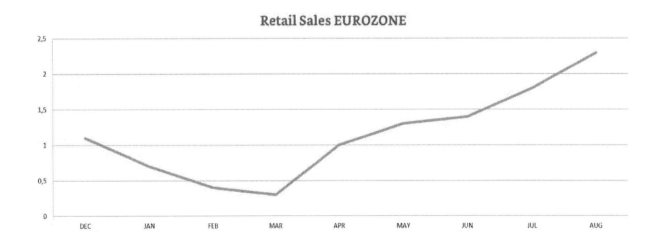

Figure 26 - Retail Sales Eurozone

From the graphs above, we can easily see that from March to August, inflation in the United States has remained practically unchanged, while Eurozone consumptions, in the last five months, have progressively increased.

Graphs are also useful for comparing the data of two or more economies, such as the Retail Sales in figure 27, in order to check which of them has had a better trend.

Figure 27 - Retail Sales, USA and Eurozone

In this way it becomes easier and faster to analyse the data of two economies that interest us. In fact, in this case, we can immediately see that up to March the American data is better than the Eurozone one, while from April to August the exact opposite happens.

However, even more can be done. In fact, if from the data of an economy we subtract those of the other, what we get is a graph of even greater visual impact. In figure 28 you can see the Retail Sales of the United States and the Eurozone, but this time as a difference.

Figure 28 - Retail Sales, USA - Eurozone

The trend of the two data is very clear in this graph. The rise up to March, which, as already mentioned, indicates a better American data than the Eurozone one, and then the decline with the Eurozone data that grows more.

Another example in Figure 29, with the Canadian and US Unemployment Rate.

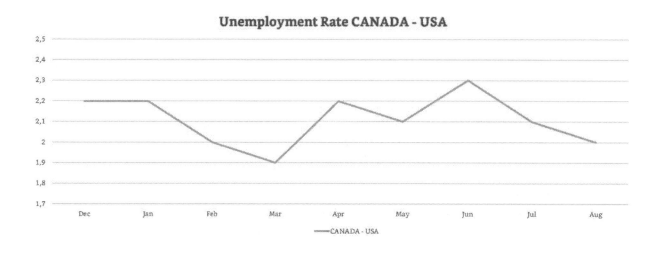

Figure 29 - Unemployment Rate, Canada - USA

Here too the trend of the two data is very clear. In fact, we can see an initial drop, with the Canadian Unemployment Rate data being better than the American one, a central phase where the inverse occurs with the graph rising, and a final part where again it is the Canadian data that improves more than the American one.

It is all a matter of organisation of data and learning to read it in a way that is comprehensible for you. Then, the data must be evaluated together with the chart of the relative currency pair. Let us look at an example regarding this, which uses Eur-Usd.

Below, in figures 30, 31, 32 and 33 are graphs of GDP, Unemployment rate, Manufacturing PMI and Retail Sales for the Eurozone and the US, constructed by subtracting the US data from the Eurozone one. So, if the graph of a data goes up, except for the Unemployment rate where the opposite is true, it means that the Eurozone has appreciated relative to the US. If the graph goes down, then the US has appreciated more than the Eurozone.

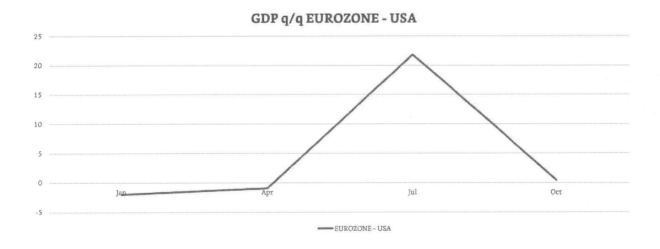

Figure 30 - Gross Domestic Product, Eurozone - USA

Unemployment rate EUROZONE - USA

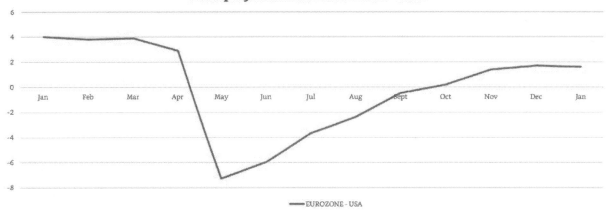

Figure 31 - Unemployment Rate, Eurozone - USA

Manufacturing PMI EUROZONE - USA

Figure 32 - Manufacturing PMI, Eurozone - USA

This period is certainly unique, as Covid-19 has affected the entire world. This can also be seen in the data for the spring months (i.e., look at how the Unemployment rate changed from April to May). However, what emerges from the graphs above and below is that in the second half of 2020, the US economy appreciated over the eurozone economy.

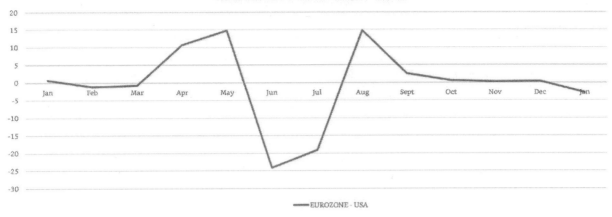

Figure 33 - Retail Sales, Eurozone - USA

In fact, the charts for GPD (although the Q4 2020 data is missing, it will be released in late January for the US and early February for the Eurozone), manufacturing and retail sales have all fallen in recent months, while the one concerning unemployment rates has risen.

After the "earthquake" caused by the pandemic, the US economy practically made up for what it had lost in the middle months of the year to the Eurozone economy.

This, then, is what emerges from an analysis of four of the main macroeconomic data. Now we have to look at the chart of Eur-Usd, to see if the trend has respected the analysis made above. Figure 34 represents the chart from the previous year of the currency pair.

The Eur-Usd trend is bullish since mid-May, from time to time interspersed with more or less long phases of sideways movements. This is particularly the case since the end of October, and does not agree with the analysis

105

of macroeconomic data.

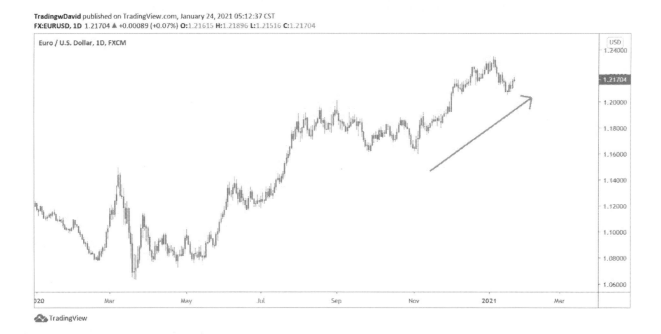

Figure 34 - Eur-Usd daily chart (TradingView.com)

Thus, it can be argued that the Eur-Usd exchange rate level is incorrect, it should be lower.

Important! Do not forget that this is only one part of the analysis, other aspects such as central bank policies (their forecasts), QE, socio-political events, etc. have to be taken into account. The picture that we get at the end may well be different.

SOME COMMENTS PART 1

CHAPTER 16

We have seen fundamental supports and resistances, and how to analyse a currency pair through macroeconomic data. Before understanding how to combine everything through the study of some currency pairs, I want to make some initial considerations. Below, we can see the Eur-Usd daily chart (figure 35).

Figure 35 - Eur-Usd daily chart (TradingView.com)

When we draw the fundamental supports and resistances, we have to take into account some aspects. A decision, like the interest rate cut or rise, might be known days or weeks before it happens and it might already be priced into the market. Furthermore, we must also bear in mind the nature of that decision.

Look at the Eur-Usd chart, to the two hikes in US interest rates in March and June 2017. As we can see, the currency pair, rather than decreasing as it was logical to expect, has risen. Why?

The answer is simple: not because the three rate hikes for the year 2017 announced by Janet Yellen, as chair of the Fed (still until February 2018), were well known months before, but because it was not their purpose to put a brake on a galloping American economy. They have been made to reduce the liquidity that has been created with Quantitative Easing (the same process will most likely see the European Union becoming the protagonist in the future).

Not only that, if we look at the day of the first interest rate hike, March 15, on the Eur-Usd chart has also formed a tall daily green candle. In this circumstance, Investors expected some more indication from Yellen, or perhaps an intervention more capable of absorbing excess liquidity. The silence of the Fed Chair in this sense has brought disappointment among the investors who have, thus, chosen to sell Dollars.

We have to therefore always take into account all the aspects, weigh every word said or not said by the presidents of central banks because they are the main market movers in Forex, the largest currency manipulators with their decisions on monetary policy.

I understand that anyone trying for the first time to read currencies in this way might view them as somewhat complicated. This was the case for me as well, besides the fact that my English at the time was not even remotely good.

As I always say, to become an engineer requires several years of study and practice. To become a pianist ten years of conservatory and exercises every day for hours. I do not see why with trading it should be different. You have to see trading as a business. With time and practice, a "fundamental" reading of the currency market will become simple and natural.

Second consideration. Here again, I start by showing a chart: that of Usd-Cad (figure 36).

Figure 36 - Usd-Cad daily chart (TradingView.com)

The chart is the same we have seen two chapters ago. The currency pair has rebounded in recent weeks from the August lows, returning to the levels of the first of two rate hikes made by the Bank of Canada.

Macroeconomic conditions have not changed from August to today (beginning of December 2017). So, at these levels, the US Dollar has a value too high compared with the Canadian homonym. But what the analysis does not tell us is the timing of the bearish entry on Usd-Cad. We look at the chart a month later (figure 37).

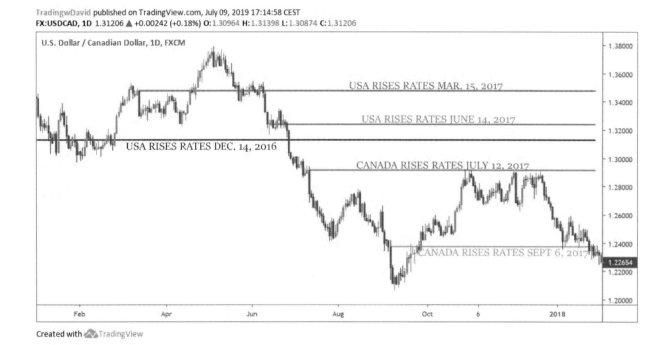

Figure 37 - Usd-Cad daily chart (TradingView.com)

As we can see, Usd-Cad initially drops but then starts to move sideways in a range of about 230 pips, forming what in technical analysis is called "rectangle."

I know that if the initial conditions do not change, the currency pair

110

will have to fall and return to a correct price. What I do not know is when it will.

So, the fundamental analysis gives me a background situation of a currency pair, tells me which of the two currencies is stronger, if the current price is correct or not but does not tell me when to open a position, that is, the timing of the market entry.

In two other charts that we have already seen, Aud-Usd (figure 38) and Nzd-Usd (figure 39), we can notice how prices can go in excess even long before returning to their correct values. So, it is not enough there is an excess of price to open a trade.

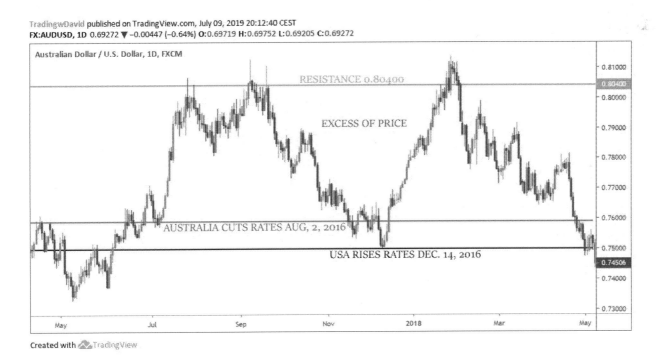

Figure 38 - Aud-Usd daily chart (TradingView.com)

For the sake of clarity, I removed the lines of the rate hikes in the United States in 2017. As we can see, a greater or lesser extent, the two currency

111

pairs have exceeded in price. The latest rate cuts in Australia and New Zealand represent significant levels beyond which we have, in fact, excesses of price.

Figure 39 - Nzd-Usd daily chart (TradingView.com)

But how do we understand when to open a position as suggested by the fundamental analysis? Let's see it in the next chapter!

SUBJECTIVE PROBABILITY

CHAPTER 17

Opening a trade, just because a pattern on the chart tells us we should, is a bad way to trade. I do not see technical analysis as the solution but as the problem. We need to identify sensitive levels for the currency pair to open our position.

As I said previously, we have to use the subjective probability, that I repeat, is the numeric measure of chance (probability) that reflects the degree of a personal belief in the likelihood of an occurrence.

Subjective probability judgments are people's evaluations of the probability of uncertain events or outcomes. It contains no formal calculations and only reflects the subject's opinions and past experience.

It is widely believed that subjective probabilities are the foundation for common errors and biases observed in the market. That does not surprise me, given how many losing traders there are, and the ignorance (understood as lack of knowledge) that hovers around trading.

All of you know who Warren Buffett is. What few people know is that

Buffet's decision process is an exercise in subjective probability. Buffet uses the "risk arbitrage" ("*risk arbitrage is something I have been doing for forty years now*").

And if we deepen our knowledge of the Oracle of Omaha, we can see quite clearly that Buffett's risk arbitrage estimates are subjective probabilities. You can read more about it in the book "*The Warren Buffett Portfolio – Mastering the Power of the Focus Investment Strategy.*"

Okay, back to business. So, how can we use subjective probability in order to find the market entry?

Let's start by saying that subjective probability differs from trader to trader. This is due to the fact that traders have different opinions and experiences.

Precisely, it is experience, which, together with the knowledge of the currency pair, which will be our best advisors. They are the ones who will give us those sensitive points that get the highest odds of success for our market entry.

Over time we need to understand how a specific currency pair behaves, the movements it makes and how it does them. That will ensure we have clearer vision, in order to be able to identify levels that are statistically better for opening up a trade.

Yes, I know, all this seems complicated to you. But trading is not as easy as you are led to believe, in particular by certain advertisements and websites. Know that my results come from much study and practice. There was, and still is a lot of work behind the scenes.

You can get excellent results from Forex, maybe even better than my own, but only if you work hard and follow what I am going to teach you in this book.

You need to change your mentality and become a new person. Look at Forex, and more generally trading, with different eyes. The most important thing about a trader is their mentality. The trader must have an entrepreneurial mindset and see trading as an entrepreneurial business.

Let me give an example to complete this concept. Below, we can see the Eur-Usd 4 daily chart (figure 40).

Figure 40 - Eur-Usd 4 daily chart (TradingView.com)

You will certainly have noticed how the X.XX20 levels (i.e. 1.0920, 1.1020, 1.1120, 1.1220, etc.) for EUR-USD are sensitive price levels. This aspect could be exploited, in particular, to open short-term trades (but not only).

That's just one aspect, a characteristic of Eur-Usd. Once you understand how the currency pair moves, when you know it perfectly, you will no longer even need to open the chart to decide your trade.

And the Forex world is full of these aspects; you have to learn to know each currency pair inside out. Below is another example. In figure 41, we can see the Usd-Jpy daily chart.

Figure 41 - Usd-Jpy daily chart (TradingView.com)

I have highlighted the first three sensitive areas above the price (we can call them also with the acronym PRZ, Potential Reversal Zone). For several reasons, we intend to sell the currency pair; we just have to decide at which level to open the trade.

For sure, the last thing to do is to open a trade at the current price just because our analysis said that the currency pair has to rise or fall.

Our analysis tells us where the currency pair will go in the middle to long-term (if the conditions do not change), but in the short term, as I already said, it is always speculation that moves it.

We can easily see that the three areas have different colours. I used different colours to help you understand better the different probabilities of the price hitting those areas and reversing the trend.

Assuming that the initial conditions that led us to decide to sell the currency pair have not changed, the first area (colour orange), is the one that is most likely to be hit by the price. Conversely, it is also the one with the lowest odds of seeing a price reversing the trend.

With the second area (yellow colour), the odds of the price hitting it decreases, but if this happens, the probability of seeing a trend reversal increases. The third area (green colour) is the one with a high likelihood of seeing a reversal of the trend. On the other hand, however, the probability of the price hitting it is low. If the price goes beyond the green area, then we should review our analysis because we probably did something wrong.

There is no rule to determine where to enter the sell order of Usd-Jpy (or any other currency pair we are trading). Everything depends on our experience and the probability that we give to the price of reaching a certain level.

If our analysis is correct, in one of those three coloured areas, it is highly probable that the price will start a bearish movement. It is there that we have to insert the sell order. But which of the three levels to choose?

In addition to our analysis, experience and knowledge of Usd-Jpy, it can be helpful to take a look at volatility. If the volatility is high, the price will probably rise above the first level, the orange one (and it is not said that it cannot overcome also the second level). If instead, we are in the presence of low volatility, the first level is where, most likely, we should sell the currency pair.

So, we wait until Usd-Jpy reaches the first area (orange) and there, we will evaluate the strength of the trend, the volatility, and whether to open all the position, just a part of it, or keep waiting.

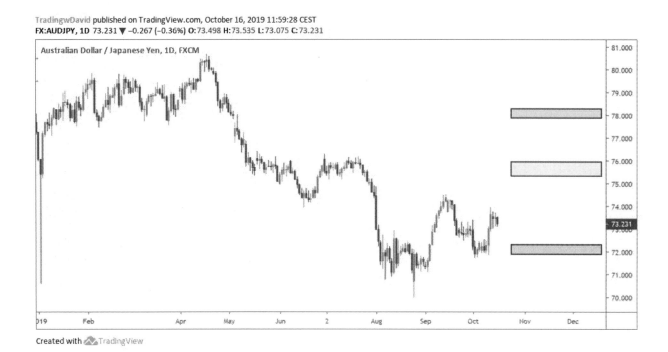

Figure 42 - Aud-Jpy daily chart (TradingView.com)

Okay, it is time to tell you that there is a way to find sensitive areas of a market even without a lot of experience. I am going to explain this method using the above Aud-Jpy daily chart (figure 42).

On the chart, we can see highlighted the first two sensitive areas above the price (yellow and green), and the first one below it (grey).

And what about the target profit?

First, you need to know when to take your profit before opening the trade (decide that in your trading plan). It has to be a statistically achievable profit, and then, just like you did with the market-entry, use subjective probability.

Figure 43 - Aud-Jpy daily chart with Volume Profile (TradingView.com)

So, let's see how a beginner can find these sensitive areas. We have to use a tool called Volume Profile. What is Volume Profile?

Volume Profile is an advanced charting study that shows the traded volume amount of an asset, over a specified period at certain price levels. We immediately see the Volume Profile applied to the chart of Aud-Jpy (figure 43 above).

There are three different types of volume profile which we can use in our trading. These types are not so different in what they do. Their difference is how they show it on the chart.

We use the basic Volume Profile tool, the VPVR (Volume Profile Visible Range). It helps to display the amount of volume occurring at certain price levels. The Volume Profile is basically a study of the volume based on price; it is a bit different when compared to the regular volume based on the time-frame, which you usually see below the chart.

Let's briefly take a look at the main features. Volume profile shows volume data as a histogram on the right (nothing forbids you from putting it on the left hand side if you prefer) with different colours. The zone with colours yellow and blue is called Value Area (VA) and is where 70% of the volume is located in the Volume Profile.

The green line high (VAH or Value Area High) is the highest point in the Value Area section. The green line low (VAL or Value Are Low) is the lowest point in the Value Area section. Usually, they are supports and resistances.

Every single bar on the histogram of the Volume Profile is called Node.

We can find High Volume Nodes (HVN), points in volume profile where there is a significantly higher volume than average, and Low Volume Nodes (LVN), points in volume profile where there is a significantly lower volume than average.

The highest volume node on the volume profile is called Point of Control (POC). It is the "gravity centre" in the chart because it is an important retest point. The price tends to back at that level.

If we take the chart of Aud-Jpy (figure 44), we can see that the three areas highlighted coincide with the POC and the HVN.

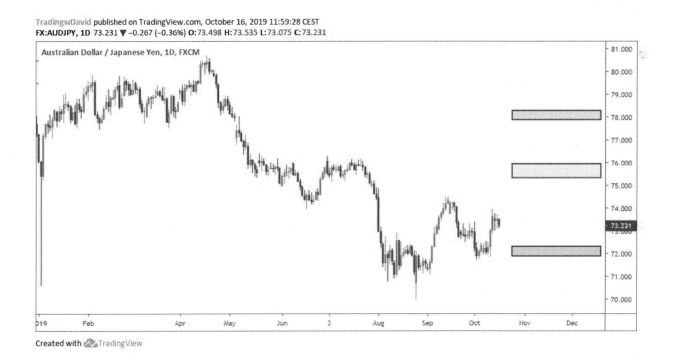

Figure 44 - Aud-Jpy daily chart (TradingView.com)

Below, we can see the chart but with the same areas highlighted and the Volume Profile added in (figure 45).

Figure 45 - Aud-Jpy daily chart with Volume Profile (TradingView.com)

There would still be a lot to say about the Volume Profile, but it would not affect our purpose. If you have doubts, curiosity or questions to ask me, you can contact me via e-mail, social networks or through my website.

What you have seen is how to find sensitive areas of the price thanks to a sharp increase in volumes. Volume Profile helps to show traders where to enter and exit a trade. With time you will learn to recognise these areas even without the Volume Profile on the chart.

Two last things. Firstly, if the time period on the chart increases, the Volume Profile changes (Value Area and, most likely, the POC). The same is the case if it decreases.

This is because, of course, if there are more or less trading days, there will also be more or less volumes (and differently distributed ones). I generally use the chart with the last 9-10 months on it.

Secondly, before you ask, is terrible news. It is rare to find the Volume Profile for free on the various available platforms. To use Volume Profile in TradingView, you need a pro account or a free trial.

In conclusion, no method in the world can give us a 100% chance of winning predictions; it is all a matter of probability. In the subjective probability theory, it is up to us to analyse the hypotheses. It differs from the technical analysis that returns clear signals, but which, unfortunately, most of the times leads to a loss.

In the next two chapters we are going to get to know better the safe-haven and commodity currencies.

SAFE-HAVEN CURRENCIES

CHAPTER 18

When we trade currencies, we need to be very clear about all the strong points, but we also need to realise what we need to keep under control. Strategically, it is necessary to know what might put us in trouble, and what to do if and when this happens. For example, closing a trade even though it has not reached the stop-loss or target.

When there is fear, there is emotion. Financial markets are emotions. And if we have to classify feelings, when there is fear in the Forex market, we go emotionally on CHF and JPY, the so-called "**Safe-Haven Currencies.**" We also have to take care of the psychological aspect because, in trading, there are machines, but there are also human beings. And in the end, it all comes down to psychology, and when there is fear, the CHF and JPY are bought.

First, we have to analyse these relationships and, after, we have to improve them, taking the best points on the chart. We start by trying to read the emotions because they are the ones that can cause large movements. Then there is also the technical aspect, but this comes at a later time. We always have to keep in mind that when there are emotional difficulties, everyone goes on these two currencies.

Now, we have to ask ourselves some questions: to buy Yen, but against which currency? In what moment? Does the Swiss Franc have positive components? When is it wise to put it in the portfolio and when not?

Some aspects of CHF are quite particular. Besides being a safe-haven currency, its oscillation also brings benefits or disadvantages for its own economy, Considering that Switzerland is an exporting country.

The first step, then, to always keep always in mind, is that since Switzerland is an export-led economy, a Swiss Franc too strong will generate a lot of problems in the export. In fact, the Swiss National Bank is not very happy to see Eur-Chf below 1.10. That is one aspect, however, that when compared with all the rest, is inferior in importance, or better yet, is considered inferior in strength.

If for example, the ECB is using only 5% for the QE, it means that the ECB can use liquidity higher than the European GDP. From this, we can understand that the force of a central bank like the ECB is superior to the will of a small nation. We have to keep in mind this; we must always be clear about which are pros and cons for both economies.

We can use CHF against EUR because it has a point in its favour. It is a currency pair which does not move much in terms of volatility compared to the other currency pairs, and this puts us in a position to work it more comfortably.

Moreover, we cannot look at another currency pair with CHF (for example Usd-Chf), in the same way as Eur-Chf because there is a different basic analysis. It is true, we have CHF (safe-haven currency) on both the currency pairs, but there is also a change in conditions. On the one hand, there is the Euro and the Eurozone, which have a very close economic relationship, and for this reason, it is difficult for the Eur-Chf to move strongly.

On the other side, we have Usd-Chf that suffers more than other currency pairs because there is not a relationship between the Swiss and the US economy strong enough to control the exchange rate. So, it becomes a currency pair that suffers the effects of the stronger currency, the ones where there is much more interest.

We have to go behind the scenes of the two economies, of the two currencies that make up the currency pair. Sometimes they can be fairly complicated speeches, but this will allow us to have a broader view not only within Forex but all the financial markets as well.

As in commodity spread trading, in which we have to analyse the two legs that make up the spread, here we have to examine the two economies that make up the currency pair. The relationship between the different economies is closer the greater the force applied to the control.

In summary, Eur-Chf is very controlled because very important oscillations could undermine the Swiss exports, which would put Switzerland in great difficulty. While on Usd-Chf, fluctuations are much larger. So, if we have to move in order to protect our portfolio, it is much easier to do it on Eur-Chf where we have more "control." Usd-Chf instead undergoes more the "mathematical" differences that are created inside the Forex.

Eur-Chf is slightly anticipatory of Eur-Usd for its variables of coverage. There is a very close movement between Eur-Usd and Eur-Chf, especially in certain situations. When we arrive at important points of Eur-Chf, this can determine what might happen to Eur-Usd, even though this aspect is also slightly dictated by experience. Very often, we use Usd-Chf as a "stepchild" and opposite to the Eur-Usd. However, it is not a relationship which always remains unchanged and in all market moments.

Eur-Chf is a bit more controllable than the Yen because a movement of 300/400 pips, Eur-Chf does it in months. Eur-Jpy or Usd-Jpy can also do it in a couple of days, especially when there is a hint of a crisis. That does not mean we cannot cover ourselves by buying Yen against the Euros, US Dollar or another currency. We only have to be a little more vigilant and remaining often in front of the monitor to follow the development of the currency pair.

Numerous factors are responsible for creating the dynamics that move the Japanese Yen during periods of risk aversion. While some of these factors make sense from a fundamental perspective, others are simply speculative.

How is it possible, one wonders, that the market points to investing in the currency of a country that turns out to be the most indebted in the world (based on the debt/GDP ratio)?

Japan has always been a large exporter and has continually exported significantly more goods and services than it imports. The result has been decades of current account surpluses. Therefore, its currency is more demanded than sold.

Not only this. For the 24th consecutive year, Japan was confirmed in 2017 as the largest creditor on the planet for assets invested outside its national territory.

Many of these investments tend to get back in times of risk, due to the inverse process to the so-called "carry trade." With the carry trade (we will see it again in the next chapter) the market tends to borrow in the currencies of economies with low-interest rates, investing in currencies of economies at higher rates.

When financial, economic or political tensions explode, however, as these latter are at greater risk, the aim is to disinvest and reconvert the liquidity obtained in the initial currency.

For this reason, when there is fear, when there is risk aversion, JPY tends to be bought more than sold, becoming, in fact, a safe-haven currency just like CHF (even though the dynamics are different).

In conclusion, it is important to have CHF in our portfolio but always taken at certain levels. This allows us to cover not only the other Forex operations but also our whole portfolio. Alternatively, we can use JPY, but we must always keep in mind that while Eur-Chf is easily controllable thanks to the economic relationship between the Eurozone and Switzerland, Yen is more volatile and requires a greater presence in front of the monitor.

COMMODITY CURRENCIES

CHAPTER 19

The term **"Commodity Currencies"** refers to the currencies of the countries which are heavily dependent on the export of certain raw materials, such as crude oil, precious metals, and agricultural products. There are several commodity currencies; the most traded in the Forex market are the Canadian Dollar, Australian Dollar, and New Zealand Dollar.

Unlike other countries that export commodities, exports of these countries are an essential part of their Gross Domestic Product (GDP) annually. As such, fluctuations in value or quantity of goods exported to these countries will have a more significant impact on their currencies.

Typically, then, if the price of the raw material grows, the currency of a great exporter country will appreciate more than the other ones. However, this should be considered with caution.

The currencies are more complex representations with respect simply to a market-linked to the price of an underlying asset. The performance of a commodity currency can be influenced by several other factors independent of the commodities, especially in the short-term. One of these is the differential that may form between interest rates of these countries.

For example, those of Australia (and New Zealand) with those of Japan: in general, the capital will tend to move where the rates, and then the remuneration, are higher. It involves an appreciation of the country's currency exchange rate that is attracting more capital.

Not surprisingly one of the most currency pairs exploited by traders is precisely Jpy-Aud, which, like that of New Zealand, is a very beaten path from the **carry trade** (the speculative strategy that exploits the disparity between the cost of borrowing money where it costs less and investing it where it will make more).

AUD. Australia is the world's second-largest gold producer, after South Africa. The gold exports make up a large percentage of the GDP of the country, so the changes in gold prices will have a significant impact on the GDP of Australia and the value of its currency.

In the case in which the production of gold was to diminish, this could also cause, as a consequence, a potential weakening of the Australian Dollar. The connection between the Australian Dollar and the value of gold is used as an important indicator for the currency pair Aud-Usd.

In the daily chart below, we can see a comparison of the Gold futures contract and Aud-Usd (figure 46).

Created with TradingView

Figure 46 - Correlation Aud-Usd and Gold (TradingView.com)

Australia is not only a great producer of gold but is also a major exporter of crude oil and copper (the latter directly connected with China). To a lesser extent, it also exports meat and grains.

So, we can see well how Australia is a major exporter of commodities, in particular to China. And for this reason, the Chinese economy is connected to the Australian Dollar.

NZD. The basket of currency pairs in Forex is very wide. There are, however, very liquid currencies, which are the most traded, and some others which are less important from this point of view. The currency of New Zealand is inserted into the basket of the Majors, but for trading and the importance that it has on the Forex market, it cannot be treated like all the other Majors.

If Eur-Usd makes certain percentage movements, for a currency pair inside the New Zealand Dollar, this percentage is much higher, and it has far more significant fluctuations.

It means that the liquidity that NZD moves is much smaller and therefore much more manoeuvrable. And what is much more manoeuvrable is much less controllable for us traders. As a result, it is a very dangerous currency, far more speculative, and in many ways similar to Exotics.

We have to use this currency sparingly, and in any case only if we have the option to keep it under control and with fairly small investment percentages.

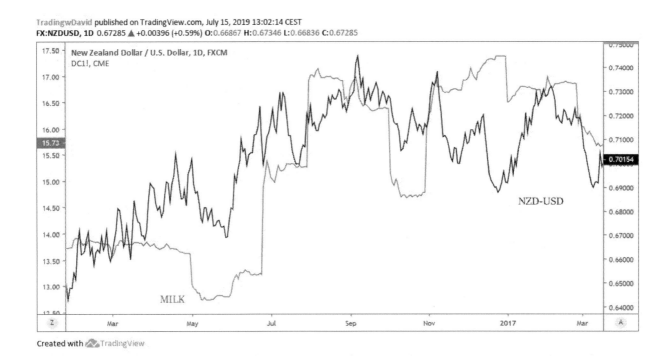

Figure 47 - Correlation Nzd-Usd and Milk (TradingView.com)

Exports for New Zealand relate to commodities such as timber, dairy and meat products. The various commodity indices have proved their value in the long-term as indicators of the value of the New Zealand Dollar.

In the daily chart in figure 47 above, we can see the correlation between the Milk futures contract and Usd-Nzd.

CAD. Canada is oil-related since it is a large producer (is among the top 5 countries in the world, although it is not part of OPEC), and is a major exporter and therefore oil is very important for its economy.

The more that price of oil grows, the more the Canadian economy will improve, and as a consequence, its currency will too, as it will get more revenue and greater profits.

The Canada supplies of oil are, above all, for the United States (with about two-thirds of exports). So, if the price of oil increases, the value of Usd-Cad decreases.

Canada is not only a major oil exporter. Another commodity that is the object of considerable export is aluminium. Canada has also had exponential growth in exports of other metals including zinc, copper and nickel.

In the chart in figure 48, we can see the inverse correlation between the Crude Oil futures contract and Usd-Cad. Here I have to make an important consideration. As we can see, not always the currency pair and oil movements are in opposite directions.

Figure 48 - Inverse correlation Usd-Cad and Crude Oil (TradingView.com)

That is because if we put the CAD, which is a strong currency, near to an even stronger currency (USD), the chance of a movement will be to the advantage of the stronger one, in this case (and at this moment, the year 2017) of the US Dollar.

This concept, I would say is almost essential; it is the basis of how we have to treat Forex. We have to look at a currency pair not as a single price, but as a clash between two economies. In this way, we can realise that putting CAD against USD or NZD is not quite the same thing.

We must, therefore, always be careful to which currency, which economy, we oppose to AUD, NZD and CAD. If we put a strong currency as AUD against an even stronger currency such as USD, the strength of the US Dollar will cancel in several cases the benefits to AUD of an increase in commodity prices. As already said, the decisions of the Fed and some macroeconomic data have a greater impact than a commodity.

On the other hand, if we compare AUD with a weaker currency (thus with an economy), the situation is more uncertain, and a rise of some commodity prices may impart new vigour to the Australian Dollar.

In the next chapter, we are going to see how we can analyse a currency pair using everything we have learnt in this book.

ANALYSIS OF A CURRENCY PAIR

CHAPTER 20

In this chapter, we will learn how to analyse a currency pair on the basis of everything we have seen in the previous pages of this book. We are going to analyse a couple of currency pairs, in order to have a correct basic view of the economies of the two countries in question.

Figure 49 - Gbp-Usd daily chart (TradingView.com)

We start with Gbp-Usd. First, let's check out the chart, which we can see above with all the most important levels (figure 49).

On June 23, 2016, with the "Brexit" referendum, the United Kingdom left the European Union, with the consequent collapse of the Pound in the following weeks.

On December 14, 2016, the United States increased interest rates by 25 basis points. Initially, macro resistance held up well, with Gbp-Usd falling and remaining below this level. Then after, the currency pair began a bullish trend.

On 2 November 2017, the United Kingdom increased the interest rates by 25 basis points to 0.50%, thus creating new macroeconomic support at 1.32500.

These are the most important macroeconomic levels. At the "technical" level, we can see static support at 1.34500, and the first resistance that the uptrend will meet at 1.41000.

So, **the first thing we always have to do** is to take the chart and highlight the key levels, both macroeconomic and deriving from the technical analysis (for the moment, in future we should highlight the zones indicated by the subjective probability).

The next step is to divide the pros and cons of the economies that make up the currency pair. I start with the **United Kingdom**.

PROS:

- Good jobs data with an increase in wages.

CONS:

- Brexit (uncertainty and high inflation);
- Prime Minister Theresa May does not have a majority in Parliament;
- Security (terrorist attacks).

The United Kingdom is experiencing a moment of uncertainty, both for what will be the effects of Brexit (it will enter into force in March 2019), and politics, with Prime Minister Theresa May who does not have a majority and has been defeated in Parliament several times.

Now, we have to do the same analysis with the **United States**, even though we have already seen it several times, and it has not changed much over time.

PROS:

- Domestic consumption-based economy;
- Currency used for international trade;
- Good data regarding employment;
- Tax cuts;
- Three projected interest rate hikes in 2018.

CONS:

- Donald Trump (Russiagate, loss of popularity, protectionist policy);
- International policy (North Korea);

- Problems with budget deficit.

The United States is continuing in economic growth, with three expected rate hikes in 2018. The only uncertainty comes from Trump and his policy.

At this point, **the second step to take** is to divide for each economy those that are the pros and cons.

So, we have to do a macroeconomic analysis, starting from the **United Kingdom** whose main macroeconomic data are reported in Table 6.

Macro-data	APR	MAY	JUN	JUL	AUG	SEP	OCT	NOV	DEC
Rate		0.25%	0.25%		0.25%	0.25%		0.50%	0.50%
Unempl. Rate	4.7%	4.6%	4.6%	4.5%	4.4%	4.3%	4.3%	4.3%	4.3%
Av. Earn.	2.3%	2.4%	2.1%	1.8%	2.1%	2.1%	2.2%	2.2%	2.5%
GDP	0.3%			0.3%			0.4%		
Manuf. PMI	54.2	57.3	56.7	54.3	55.1	56.9	55.9	56.3	58.2
CPI m/m	2.3%	2.7%	2.9%	2.6%	2.6%	2.9%	3.0%	3.0%	3.1%
Retail Sales	-1.8%	2.3%	-1.2%	0.6%	0.3%	1.0%	-0.8%	0.3%	1.1%

Constr. PMI	52.2	53.1	56.0	54.8	51.9	51.1	48.1	50.8	53.1
Service PMI	55.0	55.8	53.8	53.4	53.8	53.2	53.6	55.6	53.8

Table 6 - Great Britain macroeconomic data (2017)

Now, let's see the most important macroeconomic data of the **United States** (Table 7).

Macro-data	DEC	JAN	FEB	MAR	APR	MAY	JUN	JUL	AUG
Rate	0.75		0.75	1.00		1.00	1.25	1.25	
NFP	178K	156K	227K	235K	98K	211K	138K	222K	209K
Av. Hr. Ern.	-0.1%	0.4%	0.1%	0.2%	0.2%	0.3%	0.2%	0.2%	0.3%
Unemp. Rate	4.6%	4.7%	4.8%	4.7%	4.5%	4.4%	4.3%	4.4%	4.3%
Adv. GDP		1.9%			0.7%			2.6%	
ISM Manuf.	53.2	54.7	56	57.7	57.2	54.8	54.9	57.8	56.3
CPI m/m	0.2%	0.3%	0.6%	0.1%	-0.3%	0.2%	-0.1%	0.0%	0.1%

PPI m/m	0.4%	0.3%	0.6%	0.3%	-0.1%	0.5%	0.0%	0.1%	-0.1%
Retail Sales	0.1%	0.6%	0.4%	0.1%	-0.2%	0.4%	-0.3%	-0.2%	0.6%
Building Perm	1.20M	1.21M	1.29M	1.21M	1.26M	1.23M	1.17M	1.25M	1.22M
Existing Home Sales	5.61M	5.49M	5.69M	5.48M	5.71M	5.57M	5.62M	5.52M	5.44M

Table 7 - United States macroeconomic data (2017)

From the two tables above with the most important macroeconomic data, we can see how those of the **United Kingdom** are conflicting. GDP had modest growth in 2017. The increase in import prices, due to the depreciation of the Pound Sterling after Brexit, pushed inflation beyond the target of 2% (3.1% in November).

On the other hand, labour data are positive, with the unemployment rate falling to 4.3% in November and with recovery, in the second half of the year, of wage growth.

Analysing the data of the **United States**, there has been a continuous improvement of employment; the unemployment rate fell to 4.1%. However, new jobs are not accompanied by a sustained increase in wages.

Consumption and inflation are also rising, even though the latter remains below (although not by much) the 2% target (1.7%).

Therefore, the **third step we have to take** is to analyse the two economies through macroeconomic data. It is advisable to use data of the last 18/24 months for a more accurate analysis.

Now, to complete the analysis, we have to read the statements and minutes released by the two Central Banks, BoE and Fed. I also begin in this case from the **United Kingdom**. Below we can read the main steps of the last Monetary Policy Summary and Minutes.

"GDP grew modestly over the next few years, at a pace just above its reduced rate of potential. Consumption growth remained sluggish in the near-term before rising, in line with household incomes.

Global growth has remained strong. Domestically, some activity indicators suggest GDP growth in Q4 might be slightly softer than in Q3.

Net trade was bolstered by the strong global expansion and the past depreciation of sterling. Business investment, while affected by uncertainties around Brexit, was projected to continue to grow at a modest pace.

Unemployment was expected to remain low throughout the three-year forecast period, and domestic inflationary pressures were projected to pick up gradually as remaining spare capacity was absorbed and wage growth recovered.

Developments regarding the United Kingdom's withdrawal from the European Union – and in particular the reaction of households, businesses and asset prices to them – remain the most significant influence on, and source of uncertainty about, the economic outlook."

Now the **United States** with the main steps from the last Statement issued by the FOMC.

"The labour-market has continued to strengthen and that economic activity has been rising at a solid rate. Averaging through hurricane-related fluctuations, job gains have been solid, and the unemployment rate declined further.

Household spending has been expanding at a moderate rate. On a 12-month basis, both overall inflation and inflation for items other than food and energy have declined this year and are running below 2 per cent.

The Committee continues to expect that, with gradual adjustments in the stance of monetary policy, economic activity will expand at a moderate pace and labour-market conditions will remain strong."

The fourth and last step we have to take to complete the analysis of a currency pair is to read the last Statement and Minutes of each Central Bank, and highlight the most significant steps, just like I did above.

Now we have a complete view of Gbp-Usd, which means we can draw our conclusions on the basis of which we will make our decisions.

The **United Kingdom** is experiencing a period of uncertainty after the referendum that has stated the exit from the European Union, and this was reflected in the Pound Sterling as well. This uncertainty, that is also political, concerning Prime Minister Theresa May is due to the fact that she no longer held a majority in Parliament after the last elections took place on June 8, 2017.

Macroeconomic data depict a low-growth English economy, with GDP in decline compared with the previous years. Inflation has jumped over 3% for the devaluation of the Pound Sterling. The Bank of England raised interest rates by 25 basis points in November 2017, with also the aim of curbing inflation.

On the other hand, employment data improved, with the unemployment rate declining by 0.5% in 2017 to 4.3%; data that has been accompanied in the second half of the year by a recovery in wages.

I went to see the pre-Brexit macroeconomic data (not shown), and it has only gotten better in terms of employment (in June 2016 the unemployment rate was at 5%). Retail sales remained almost unchanged, while, as mentioned, GDP declined.

The **United States**, on the other hand, continues to expand at a moderate pace, with labour data remaining strong, and a continuously falling unemployment rate at 4.1%, although a sustained increase in wages does not yet accompany it. There is, however, an increase in consumer spending.

Inflation is on the rise, and at the end of 2017, after the three rate hikes, it was at 1.7%, just below the 2% target. GDP is growing beyond the estimates that have been revised upwards in the last Economic Projection at 2.5% for both 2017 and 2018. Three rate hikes are confirmed for 2018.

In conclusion: the strong rise of speculative origin for Gbp-Usd, is not reflected in macroeconomic analysis. The American economy remains stronger than the English one and with fewer uncertainties. However, I consider it very likely that the Dollar will continue to depreciate, due to the protectionist policy that Trump intends to adopt.

So, at the moment, rather than looking for a level where to open short positions, I would open a **bullish short-term trade on the Pound Sterling** which, when it moves, has no problem doing it even for 200-300 pips. In this way, I try to exploit a probable weakening of the Dollar. However, in the **medium to long-term, Gbp-Usd is expected to fall**.

As we can see, a correct analysis from all points of view can also lead us to open a short-term trade against what the fundamental analysis says.

After the analysis of Gbp-Usd, let's proceed with the second currency pair: Eur-Aud. As a first step, replicating the same procedure seen with Gbp-Usd, let us take a look at the chart, which I have highlighted with the most important levels (figure 50).

Figure 50 - Eur-Aud daily chart (TradingView.com)

On August 2, 2016, the Royal Bank of Australian cut interest rates by 25 basis points, but despite this, for several months the currency pair moved below this level. This is due to the strong liquidity injection of the ECB, which is able to devalue the Euro.

It is no coincidence that from the 26th of July 2017, the day when for the first time Mario Draghi, ECB chairman, talked about the possible termination of QE by the end of the year, the Euro started to rise against all the other currencies, including the Australian Dollar.

Indeed, Eur-Aud returned above the macroeconomic level created by the rates cut of the Reserve Bank of Australia, which, from that moment on, became strong support.

The currency pair continued to rise by breaking the resistance in the 1.52000 area. The currency pair continued to rise by breaking the resistance (now support) in the 1.52000 area, and that just a couple of days before the writing of this chapter, it was tested.

We have different dynamics to analyse, but let's proceed in order. The next step is to divide the pros and cons of each economy that makes up the currency pair. I start with the **Eurozone**.

PROS:

- Good data regarding employment;
- GDP revised up at 2.4% this year;
- The end of QE (in a soft way).

146

CONS:

- Immigration;
- Security (terrorist attacks);
- Several political elections in 2018 (in particular Italy, Hungary and Poland);
- Different economies inside;
- Low Inflation.

For the Eurozone, the end of Quantitative Easing should lead to an appreciation of the Euro. Added to this is an economy that grows with GDP revised upwards this year. There are still differences between the countries within it that show structural problems. There is always a constant danger of terrorist attacks. In 2018 there will be several political elections.

Now we have to do the same thing with **Australia**, even though we have already seen it several times and it has not changed much over time.

PROS:

- Growth in GDP and it is expected to be 2.8% this year (a bit lower than 3% of some months before but still over the initial 1.8%);
- Good data regarding employment.

CONS:

- Moderate consumptions;

- Exports-based economy. It depends on other economies (China) and the prices of commodities;
- An appreciating exchange rate would complicate growth.

Australia is showing signs of recovery with a GDP higher than initial estimates and excellent data on employment. Low consumption which still does not strongly stimulate growth. The economy is always based on commodities and commercial relations with China.

A weak Dollar would favour an increase in commodity prices but, at the same time, would strengthen the currency pair Aud-Usd, complicating growth.

Now, we have to see the main macroeconomic data of the two economies. We can find in the table below those relating to the **Eurozone** (Table 8).

Macro-data	APR	MAY	JUN	JUL	AUG	SEP	OCT	NOV	DEC
Rate	0.0%		0.0%	0.0%		0.0%	0.0%		0.0%
Unempl. Rate	9.5%	9.5%	9.3%	9.3%	9.1%	9.1%	9.1%	8.9%	8.8%
GDP		0.5%			0.6%			0.6%	
Zew	19.5	20.6	18.6	17.5	10.0	17.0	17.6	18.7	17.4

Flash PMI	56.8	57.0	57.3	56.8	57.4	58.2	58.6	60.0	60.6
CPI y/y	1.9%	1.4%	1.3%	1.3%	1.5%	1.5%	1.4%	1.5%	
Retail Sales	0.7%	0.3%	0.1%	0.4%	0.5%	-0.3%	-0.5%	0.7%	-1.1%

Table 8 - Eurozone macroeconomic data (2017)

Below, the main **Australian** macroeconomic data (Table 9).

Macro-data	APR	MAY	JUN	JUL	AUG	SEP	OCT	NOV	DEC
Rate	1.50%	1.50%	1.50%	1.50%	1.50%	1.50%	1.50%	1.50%	1.50%
Unemp. Change	60.9K	37.4K	42.0K	14.0K	27.9K	54.2K	19.8K	3.7K	61.6K
Unemp. Rate	5.9%	5.7%	5.5%	5.6%	5.6%	5.6%	5.5%	5.4%	5.4%
GDP			0.3%			0.8%			0.6%
CPI q/q	0.5%			0.2%			0.6%		
Retail Sales	-0.1%	-0.1%	1.0%	0.6%	0.3%	0.0%	-0.6%	0.0%	0.5%

| Building Appr. | 8.3% | -13.4% | 4.4% | -5.6% | 10.9% | -1.7% | 0.4% | 1.5% | 0.9% |

Table 9 - Australia macroeconomic data (2017)

From the two tables above, we can see that the **Eurozone** data show an improvement but that it is still slow. Good data regarding employment, with the unemployment rate falling by 1% in 2017. Retail sales, however, has practically remained steady in 2017 (+0.1% the balance of data released from December 2016 to December 2017).

Business confidence, as shown by the Zew index, is growing slightly but remains below the long-term average of 23.7 points. Consumer confidence is growing (data not reported) and in December 2017 has returned to positive after more than ten years.

As for **Australia**, in the last year, there has been a significant improvement in the labour-market with an unemployment rate dropped by half a percentage point from April to December. Inflation remains slightly below the target while the Retail Sales figure does not yet show a marked recovery in consumption.

The final phase of the analysis concerns the reading of the last Statement and Minutes of the two Central Banks. Let's start with the **Eurozone**; we find below the most significant steps of the last Statement released by the ECB.

"Regarding non-standard monetary policy measures, we confirm that

from January 2018 we intend to continue to make net asset purchases under the asset purchase programme (APP), at a monthly pace of €30 billion, until the end of September 2018, or beyond, if necessary.

The incoming information, including our new staff projections, indicates a strong pace of economic expansion and a significant improvement in the growth outlook. This assessment is broadly reflected in the December 2017 Eurosystem staff macroeconomic projections for the Euro area. These projections foresee annual real GDP increasing by 2.4% in 2017, 2.3% in 2018, 1.9% in 2019 and 1.7% in 2020. Compared with the September 2017 ECB staff macroeconomic projections, the outlook for real GDP growth has been revised up substantially.

Private consumption is underpinned by ongoing employment gains, which are also benefiting from past labour-market reforms, and by rising household wealth

Business investment continues to strengthen on the back of very favourable financing conditions, rising corporate profitability and strengthening demand."

From the last Statement released by the **Reserve Bank of Australia**:

"The outlook for non-mining business investment has improved further, with the forward-looking indicators being more positive than they have been for some time. Increased public infrastructure investment is also supporting the economy.

Employment growth has been strong over 2017 and the unemployment rate has declined. Employment has been rising in all states and has been accompanied by a rise in labour force participation.

There are reports that some employers are finding it more difficult to hire workers with the necessary skills. However, wage growth remains low, and this means there is uncertainty in the outlook for household consumption. Household incomes are growing slowly, and debt levels are high.

The Australian Dollar remains within the range that it has been in over the past two years. An appreciating exchange rate would be expected to result in a slower pick-up in economic activity and inflation than currently forecast."

Now that we have finished our analysis, we can draw the appropriate conclusions.

In conclusion: both economies are registering higher growth than the estimates a year earlier. Data regarding employment (even though we have two very different rates of unemployment) are improving, but consumer spending is running late.

The difference is the end of the ECB's Quantitative Easing which has given, and will give, a strong boost to the Euro. That is why **Eur-Aud is expected to rise in the medium to long-term**.

However, the probable devaluation of the US Dollar (Trump's protectionist policy) and the increase in the price of gold should bring benefits to the Australian Dollar in the short-term, with a decrease of the currency pair.

In the case of a decrease of Aud-Eur below 1.48000 (the most recent cut in interest rates of the Reserve Bank of Australia), it would create an excellent opportunity to open a long position on the currency pair, but we are still very far away from this. A good strategy is to place a spy-order in the area 1.52000 (sensitive area); As it is in fact very likely that Eur-Aud will start a new bullish phase from that level.

At the end of this chapter, I report the four key steps to make a correct analysis of a currency pair, to understand which of the two currencies (and therefore economies) is the strongest.

1. **First step**: take the chart and highlight the key levels, both macroeconomic and sensitive for the market (at the beginning, you can draw static supports and resistances).

2. **Second step**: highlight the pros and cons of each of the economies that make up the currency pair.

3. **Third step**: analyse the two economies through their macroeconomic data. I advise taking data from at least the last 18/24 months for a better analysis.

4. **Fourth step**: go to read the last Statement and Minutes, and underline the most significant steps, just as I did in the analyses we have seen in this chapter.

What we have seen explained, in its various phases, is the correct way to analyse a currency pair that, as I have already mentioned, is nothing more than comparing two economies. That is how investment banks operate.

They do not use technical analysis; you will not see charts with indicators on their monitors. They do not use trading systems or expert advisors attached on Metatrader platform.

Furthermore, it is clear that a significant part of the entire process of analysis is also given by the experience in the field, and this is an aspect that is difficult to teach. At best, I can give advice dictated by my own experience.

The next two chapters will cover some aspects concerning the portfolio, both in terms of diversification and money management.

DIVERSIFICATION OF PORTFOLIO
CHAPTER 21

My first years in Forex were a disaster; I was great at losing money. I had studied all sorts of indicators and oscillators. I had studied computers at university, so I had created Expert Advisors (automated strategies "attached" to Metatrader platform) increasingly complex because they worked for me while I was enjoying the money earned in some Caribbean paradise.

Nothing could be more wrong; I ignored a very important fact: markets change depending on the moment. They do not always move in the same way. There will be more volatile periods and others less so, periods of trend and others in congestion.

An example that I often make is comparing this to going all-year-round in the same clothes. Seasons change just like markets do, and it is not possible (or at least wise) to go dressed in the same way throughout the year, just like we cannot use a strategy profitably in every situation of the market.

What does it mean to always operate with the same strategy? A strategy may have been good for years, but within these years it will have favourable moments, and others less so. Working with a single strategy means having great experience and knowing when to use it and when to not. It means being very disciplined and being prepared to withstand possible negative situations, even for a long period of time.

Operating with a portfolio means covering ourselves; learning to develop more strategies on the market so that we can ensure we overcome any and every situation – since one strategy can be causing trouble whilst another giving a profit, it is essential, therefore, to have equilibrium in our portfolio.

For example, we may be in trend, and we can exploit it with the spot Forex by buying or selling a currency pair. If the market moves sideways, instead, we can be non-directional using the options on the currency futures.

We saw another example of this in one of the previous chapters, with the safe-haven currencies. We can balance our portfolio using CHF or JPY to cover some more aggressive trade.

These and other measures, all put together, create a portfolio. The portfolio tends to protect us in times of trouble (doing the proper balancing). This concept is the basis of how to manage our money and how to invest our savings. I have not yet found the perfect strategy that works for every occasion, but I suspect that it does not exist.

In this way, we get more cards to play, we compensate those times when a strategy loses a bit of effectiveness or has fewer opportunities. In that case, we can use another strategy, so we have a diversification of portfolio always effective, and when we are losing on the one hand, we are gaining from another. That is, in my opinion, the perfect structure to get us comfortable in every market situation.

I will end this short chapter by explaining how I divided my Forex portfolio, just to give you an idea of how it works. It is divided into three parts:

- 10% for intraday operations. It is rare, but occasionally I also make "hit-and-run" trades, in particular with NFP;
- 75% for medium-term operations following the fundamental analysis of the currencies;
- 15% in liquidity.

Withdrawals: (for all the assets). I withdraw monthly 100% of profits obtained from intraday operations, at least 50% of those obtained with the medium-term activity, and I leave on the account the gains got in the long-term savings plan (that does not concern Forex).

Every two or three months, I make a rebalancing of the whole portfolio with percentages that remain unchanged.

MONEY MANAGEMENT
CHAPTER 22

Money management is the mainstay and the centre pin of our investments, essential for all our trading. Few traders adopt proper money management; for this reason, approximately 85% of traders lose all their money in a few weeks.

Money management consists in **position size**, which identifies the part of the equity to be invested in each trade and the allocation of money on the various assets in the portfolio, and **risk management**, which analyses the risk linked to the position taken in the market. You can find more information about this in my book: "**Behavioural Finance - Psychology and Money Management.**"

Every trader who gets steady profits over time follows the rules of money management in an absolutely rigid way. It is essential to know from the very beginning of our trading business how much percentage of our equity to allocate to each trade. Our first thought should be directed to the protection and preservation of the money but only after its maximisation.

One of the adages of Wall Street says: "*cut the losses short and let the profits run.*" I am always impressed by the fact that before, it refers to keeping small losses, and only later does it worry about letting profits run. money protection must be our first thought because being a trader includes making losses. Anyone who tells you that he has never lost yet has never protected his money is telling you a lie.

If we are able, then, to keep small the losses and let the profits run, as the saying goes, we will be sure to make a profit over the long-term. To do this, we have to analyse the market correctly, so that even before we open a trade, we can be confident in our action plan. This way we will know how much we can lose and will not find ourselves in trouble when we face a negative situation. The more we are aware of how much we could lose, the more stress-free and tranquil the trade will be.

Trading is an entrepreneurial activity, something that has to give us an income, but at the same time must not be a burden, or worsen our quality of life. The most important aspect of trading is risk control. To do this, I repeat, we need to have a well-defined trading plan which we will always stick to and respect.

As I said, I like to set up operations wide-ranging, that is, making sure that, even though there is a movement against my position, this does not put me in trouble, and I can manage the operation with confidence.

So before, I insert a first order for testing the market, a "spy-order" usually of a small amount (at most 1/3 of the entire order), of course, always proportionate to the equity. Then, I insert a higher "primary-order", concerning the size, just to rebalance the average price and be able to manage better the operation.

But what should be the dimensions of the spy-order and primary-order? When I decide to insert a spy-order, I determine the size according to the maximum loss of the entire operation. For example, I choose to risk for every medium-term Forex trade at most 1.50% of my equity. 1.50% in turn divided into 0.75% for the spy-order, and 0.75% of the primary-order (which is closer to the stop-loss than the spy-order and which will have a greater size). However, it is just an example, and we can decide different percentages based on our risk appetite.

Money Management is an important part of the strategy. If for example, we buy a currency pair too soon, we risk getting an average price that can put us in trouble later. Be greedy and living with trading are incompatible.

Figure 51 - Aud-Usd daily chart (TradingView.com)

Let me give an example to understand how better to choose the size of the two orders. I reuse the Aud-Usd chart already seen and that, for convenience, I have placed above in figure 51.

Once we completed our analysis, we decide to sell Aud-Usd. So, we insert a spy-order at 0.80400 and a primary-order at 0.83000 with the stop-loss at 0.85000 (for both the orders). The part of the equity that we use for the medium-term operations is $ 30,000 (this is just an example).

So, using the same percentage of loss of the previous example, 0.75% of $ 30,000 is equal to $ 225.00. That means that the maximum loss for the spy-order will be $ 225.00, and the maximum loss of the primary-order will always be $ 225.00.

At this point, knowing the value of 1 pip ($ 0.10 for each $ 1,000 of investment for Aud-Usd), we can calculate the size of the two orders with a simple formula:

[1,000 * (equity * %of max loss) / pips of stop] / value of 1 pip

Concerning our example of Aud-Usd, we calculate now the size of the two orders:

Size spy-order = [1,000 * (30,000 * 0.75%) / 460] / 0.10 = 5K

Size primary-order = [1,000 * (30,000 * 0.75%) / 200] / 0.10 = 11K

So, we sell Aud-Usd with 5K at 0.80400 (the spy-order), and we insert an order to sell 12K at 0.83000 (the primary-order). The stop-loss is at 0.85000 while we identify the first target in 0.76000 area. The target must not be too ambitious, and must also be in the sensitive areas of the currency pair.

As I already said, while the stop-loss level is fixed, and at that level, we have to close the trade with no ifs or buts, before inserting the target, it is important to see how quickly the currency pair reaches the chosen level. Noteworthy is also the speed with which it moves a currency pair. If, for example, we get a profit 200/250 pips in 2-3 days, we can think of splitting the trade, that is, of closing at least a part of it.

When a movement is swift, we must always evaluate the speed and not be greedy, because as I have said, the difference between being greedy and letting the profit run is very subtle.

At this point, you must be wondering: how do I calculate the pip value of a currency pair? No problem, in Appendix A you have the answer.

What we have seen in this chapter is only a part of the money management and trading plan. If you want to know more about this subject, I suggest you read my book: "**Trading Behavioural Finance – Psychology and Money Management**." Remember that we always have to put ourselves in the best conditions to trade.

As regards the stop-loss, in the next chapter we are going to see the best way to use it.

VALUE-AT-RISK

CHAPTER 23

Value-at-Risk (VaR) measures the potential loss in value of a risky asset or portfolio over a defined period for a given confidence interval.

Thus, if the VaR on Eur-Usd is 1.81% at one-week, 95% confidence level, there is an only 5% chance that the value of Eur-Usd will drop more than 1.81% over any given week.

Value at Risk is used by commercial and investment banks to capture the potential loss in value of their traded portfolios from adverse market movements over a specified period; this can then be compared to their available capital and cash reserves to ensure that the losses can be covered without putting the firms at risk. But we use it in a different way.

We use the Value-at-Risk to decide where to set the stop-loss.

How? For example, if we decide to buy Eur-Usd (current price 1.0970), if we put a stop-loss 1.81% away from our entry price (that is, 1.0761), we will have 95% probability (theoretical) of not seeing it met by the price.

We fully understand that it is the best way to decide the stop-loss; it removes any doubts we might have and all the emotions.

Before I explain the calculation, let's take a step back and take a look at some aspects. There are three key elements of VaR:

1. a specified level of loss in value;
2. a fixed time period over which risk is assessed (1 day, 1 week, etc.);
3. a confidence interval (usually 95% or 99%).

The VaR can be specified for an individual asset, a portfolio of assets or an entire firm, and the idea behind it is volatility.

Three basic approaches are used to compute Value-at-Risk, though there are numerous variations within each approach.

- **Historical method**. It represents the simplest way of estimating the Value at Risk for many assets and portfolios. In this approach, the VaR for a portfolio is estimated by creating a hypothetical time series of returns on that portfolio, obtained by running the portfolio through actual historical data and computing the changes that would have occurred in each period.

- **Variance-Covariance method**. It assumes that the daily price returns for a given position follow a normal distribution. From the distribution of daily returns calculated from daily price series, we estimate the standard deviation. The daily Value-at-Risk VaR is simply a function of the standard deviation and the desired confidence level.

- **Monte Carlo simulation**. The approach is similar to the Historical method except for one big difference. The hypothetical data set used is generated by a statistical distribution rather than historical price levels. The assumption is that the selected distribution captures or reasonably approximates price behaviour of the assets or portfolios.

Which to use? The most robust results are likely to come from the historical method. This is because the approach is not hampered by the normal distribution assumption.

The Variance-Covariance method is the most popular approach. However, it is also the one that receives the most criticism given the normality assumption.

The Monte Carlo simulation appears to be fairly attractive, but in most simulators, the default distribution used is also normal. This essentially puts the results in the same category and range as the Variance-Covariance method.

All methods have a common base but then diverge in how they actually calculate Value-at-Risk.

They also have a common problem in assuming that the future will follow the past. This shortcoming is normally addressed by supplementing any Value-at-Risk figures with appropriate sensitivity analysis and/or stress testing.

Now, it is time to see the calculation for the Value-at-Risk. In order not to complicate the argument too much, I will use the historical method. We have to go on the investing.com website and search for the currency pair of our interest.

In this example, I use Eur-Usd (figure 52).

Figure 52 - Eur-Usd (Investing.com)

Here, we have to click on **Historical Data** (figure 53).

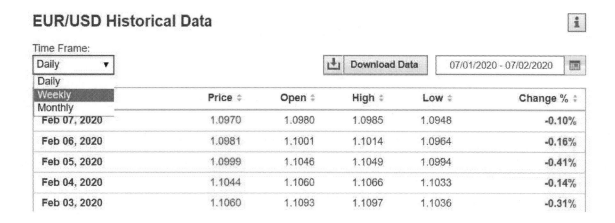

Figure 53 - Eur-Usd Historical Data (Investing.com)

On the next page, we have to select, first on the left in **Time Frame**, Weekly, and then on the right, the period of time (which has to be at least the last five years). Then, we click on **Download Data**.

Now, we have to open the file .csv with Excel. The only data we need is the Close, so we can delete everything else, as I did in figure 54.

	A	B
1	Data	Close
2		
3	Feb 02, 2020	1,097
4	Jan 26, 2020	1,1094
5	Jan 19, 2020	1,1025
6	Jan 12, 2020	1,109
7	Jan 05, 2020	1,1122
8	Dec 29, 2019	1,116
9	Dec 22, 2019	1,1177
10	Dec 15, 2019	1,1079
11	Dec 08, 2019	1,1121
12	Dec 01, 2019	1,1059
13	Nov 24, 2019	1,1017
14	Nov 17, 2019	1,1024
15	Nov 10, 2019	1,1052
16	Nov 03, 2019	1,1018
17	Oct 27, 2019	1,1167

Figure 54 - Eur-Usd weekly Close

The first thing to do is to calculate the Return of each week. The formula is simple: we have to subtract from each close the one immediately below and divide the result by the second of the two values. For the above sheet, the formula for the first Return is as follows:

=(B3-B4)/B4

167

We have to calculate the return for each close. So, it is enough to copy and paste the first formula on all the other cells, as in figure 55.

	A	B	C
1	Data	Close	Return
2			
3	Feb 02, 2020	1,097	-0,011177213
4	Jan 26, 2020	1,1094	0,006258503
5	Jan 19, 2020	1,1025	-0,005861136
6	Jan 12, 2020	1,109	-0,00287718
7	Jan 05, 2020	1,1122	-0,003405018
8	Dec 29, 2019	1,116	-0,001520981
9	Dec 22, 2019	1,1177	0,008845564
10	Dec 15, 2019	1,1079	-0,003776639
11	Dec 08, 2019	1,1121	0,005606294
12	Dec 01, 2019	1,1059	0,00381229
13	Nov 24, 2019	1,1017	-0,000634978
14	Nov 17, 2019	1,1024	-0,002533478
15	Nov 10, 2019	1,1052	0,00308586
16	Nov 03, 2019	1,1018	-0,013342885
17	Oct 27, 2019	1,1167	0,007851986

Figure 55 - Eur-Usd weekly Return

Now, we must arrange the Return column in ascending order. But doing this is not possible since the column is made up of numbers that are the result of an operation. Then, we have to copy the Return column and, after clicking with the right button in the next column, under Paste Special, choose Values. Now we can order it from the smallest to the largest value.

Furthermore, in the column alongside, we have to number the <u>Return Ascending</u> (1, 2, 3, 4, etc.) up to the penultimate value (the last is "#DIV/0!" so not valid). We can see the result of the two operations described below in figure 56.

	A	B	C	D	E
1	Data	Close	Return	Return Ascending	No.
2					
3	Feb 02, 2020	1,097	-0,011177213	-0,037981315	1
4	Jan 26, 2020	1,1094	0,006258503	-0,034068136	2
5	Jan 19, 2020	1,1025	-0,005861136	-0,032183696	3
6	Jan 12, 2020	1,109	-0,00287718	-0,0314398	4
7	Jan 05, 2020	1,1122	-0,003405018	-0,029917592	5
8	Dec 29, 2019	1,116	-0,001520981	-0,028908867	6
9	Dec 22, 2019	1,1177	0,008845564	-0,025318729	7
10	Dec 15, 2019	1,1079	-0,003776639	-0,024686809	8
11	Dec 08, 2019	1,1121	0,005606294	-0,023989096	9
12	Dec 01, 2019	1,1059	0,00381229	-0,020533881	10
13	Nov 24, 2019	1,1017	-0,000634978	-0,018438844	11
14	Nov 17, 2019	1,1024	-0,002533478	-0,018215375	12
15	Nov 10, 2019	1,1052	0,00308586	-0,01805119	13
16	Nov 03, 2019	1,1018	-0,013342885	-0,016471417	14
17	Oct 27, 2019	1,1167	0,007851986	-0,016255162	15

Figure 56 - Eur-Usd Return Ascending and Position

At this point, we have all the data to calculate the Value-at-Risk. We leave an empty column to allow for some space. At the top, we put the total data number, which is the last number in the <u>No.</u> column (figure 57).

260	Mar 01, 2015	1,0844	-0,0314398	0,02971302	258
261	Feb 22, 2015	1,1196	-0,016255162	0,030071731	259
262	Feb 15, 2015	1,1381	-0,000351339	0,031157694	<u>260</u>
263	Feb 08, 2015	1,1385	#DIV/0!	#DIV/0!	

Figure 57 - Eur-Usd last position number

Below we calculate the VaR (95%). First, we need to use the following formula to find the VaR (95%) position:

169

$$=(1-95\%)*G3$$

Where G3 is the cell number where I have put the total data number (you will use the cell you have chosen). Below the result (figure 58).

D	E	F	G	H	I
Return Ascending	No.				
-0,037981315	1		260		
-0,034068136	2				
-0,032183696	3		Var(95%)		13
-0,0314398	4				
-0,029917592	5				
-0,028908867	6				
-0,025318729	7				
-0,024686809	8				
-0,023989096	9				
-0,020533881	10				
-0,018438844	11				
-0,018215375	12				
-0,01805119	13				
-0,016471417	14				
-0,016255162	15				

Figure 58 - Eur-Usd VaR(95%)

The VaR (95%) on Eur-Usd at one-week is the figure on the left of the number 13 of the **Return Ascending** column, that is, -0.01805119, which is 1.81%.

To finish, I add that besides the Var, there is the CVar. Conditional Value-at-Risk (CVaR) is the extended risk measure of Value-at-Risk that quantifies the average loss over a specified time period of unlikely scenarios beyond the confidence level.

For example, a one-week CVaR(95%) of Eur-Usd is 2.64% means that the expected loss of the worst 5% scenarios over one week is 2.64%. Conditional Value-at-Risk is also known as Expected Shortfall.

VaR gives us a range of potential losses, whilst CVaR gives us an average of the potential loss. CVaR is generally considered a better approximation of potential losses.

The calculation is very easy. We have to divide 1 by the number of the position we have found with the VaR calculation (in the example above "13") and then multiply the result by the sum of the first 13 returns (always relative to the example) of the Return Ascending column.

The formula for the excel sheet seen above is as follows:

=(1/I5)*SUM(D3:D15)

Below, we can see the result (figure 59).

	A	B	C	D	E	F	G	H	I
1	Data	Close	Return	Return Ascending	No.				
2									
3	Feb 02, 2020	1,097	-0,011177213	-0,037981315	1		260		
4	Jan 26, 2020	1,1094	0,006258503	-0,034068136	2				
5	Jan 19, 2020	1,1025	-0,005861136	-0,032183696	3		Var(95%)	-1,81%	13
6	Jan 12, 2020	1,109	-0,00287718	-0,0314398	4		CVar(95%)	-2,64%	
7	Jan 05, 2020	1,1122	-0,003405018	-0,029917592	5				

Figure 59 - Eur-Usd, VaR and CVaR

We have seen the best way to place a stop-loss. By using the VaR or the CVar (at your discretion, personally, I use the CVaR), we will not only have found a level that has only a 5% probability of not seeing it met by the price, but we will have eliminated any type of doubt and emotion because we know we worked like an investment bank or fund.

Obviously, that percentage has to correspond to the maximum loss that we have decided in our trading plan.

SOME COMMENTS PART 2
CHAPTER 24

When we trade, unpredictability is a factor we need to consider. Even when we open a trade that seems mostly certain in all its dynamics, there is always 1-2% of our decision-making that we cannot control. We can consider every detail, gather all the information, but there is always a percentage that we cannot control. But this is the case for every investment. If we do not start from this premise, we cannot do anything.

Central banks are like CEO's of a company; and all of them believe that their company is the best. If in our analyses and considerations something unforeseen happens to come about, nothing can be done about it. We simply have to accept the change and remember that the stop-loss will limit our loss. In any case, by remaining faithful to the established plan, we have nonetheless done a proper analysis.

Now, I will talk about correlations again briefly. I have said, and you know, that I never take into account the correlations with other currencies in Forex, especially in the medium to long-term. Because doing so, we insert into a relationship between two economies, a third economy. And if this third economy changes, our entire analysis changes, essentially becoming invalid.

Correlations between currencies are an instrument that is convenient for us when everything goes well, but it causes us problems at the moment they change. We obviously cannot know when this will happen, and those are the moments in which we could really get hurt, from a financial point of view.

For this reason, I do not recommend you watch the currencies in that direction. We already have a lot to think about when we divide a currency pair in the two economies; we have enough to work with. Let's not go down a rabbit hole by inserting other currencies, because that would simply expand a problem.

When there is no clear context, it is better to take the opportunity of working with greater calm and clarity and waiting to see how the situation evolves, rather than jumping in and being immediately directional. For example, working with the options, we have the ability to manage our investment and intervene to correct it in case of wrong analysis. You can learn more about options with my books "**Options Relaxing Trading – A Complete Guide for Beginners**."

Let us remember that we are investors; we are not people who buy or sell at random. We have a portfolio that we have to maintain balanced and well built. So, we have to think before investing.

We stay far from what we cannot control (high volatility, emotionality). We are better off leaving volatile and dangerous currencies alone, and instead focus our energy on the markets that present the most interesting features to us. From my point of view, working with a currency pair that is too volatile is synonymous with handling a portfolio incorrectly. We run the risk of unbalancing it.

It is essential to be able to select the best opportunities for our trading style. For example, USA holiday = low liquidity, and this is a problem because to move a market that is less liquid is much easier for those who want to speculate with that market.

When there is uncertainty, we should stand firm and not invest. Why should we risk our money in something that we are not sure of? Better to wait for better times. When things happen that we were not expecting in our scenarios, it is better to get out and stay out; it is better to run away immediately because these are, statistically, the situations where the most money is lost. We always have to put ourselves in the best condition to work (odds of success on our side).

Similarly, we never have to run after the price; we must stay focused on our goal. When we have the odds on our side, we have to use them, but one should never run after the price; otherwise, we risk entering the market, taking the stop-loss, and seeing the currency pair go in our direction. I want to enter the market only at the price I want. I give nothing because nothing is given to me by the market.

The market is made up of expectations. For example, it is expected that the central bank will cut interest rates. If this happens, this event has already been priced into the market, and the movement will be minimal. However, if the expectation fails, the movement that will follow it will be very strong because inside there is the disappointment due to unfulfilled expectations.

As I have already said, we have to learn to know the currencies and pairs, whilst acquiring experience. For example, Gbp-Usd is a very volatile currency pair; important news is strongly speculated. It is among the most speculated currency pairs because it has, within it, two of the most treated currencies, particularly the Pound Sterling which is very volatile.

Eur-Usd has the two most liquid currencies, but Gbp-Usd is the one that creates the largest movement, as a percentage, among the "Majors." It is not a currency pair that we may directionally work with tranquillity while it becomes advantageous to work it with options (taking advantage of volatility).

Another consideration. Let's analyse a currency; I take, for example, NZD. To use it in Forex, we must put it in opposition to another currency (e.g. USD).

Important. When we contrast a weaker currency (NZD) with a stronger currency (USD), the speed at which the currency pair will move in the direction of the stronger currency is amplified, much more than the opposite. This concept is fundamental, especially when we work currency with the options.

The difficulty of a trader is to note and see the changes in scenarios on which we have based our strategy. Many times, stubbornness is what makes us say: no, this trade must go well, and it is there that we bang our head, and we get the most significant losses. But remember, we always have to be ready to modify our analysis when the scenario changes.

We must always be self-critical. Sometimes, even the positions closed in profit could have been better managed. So, we have to review everything and assess whether we have done our job correctly or if there are points where we made mistakes. For this reason, it is essential to keep a trading journal.

Always remember that in trading, the simplest things are always the best, and the ones that last the longest.

ODDS ON OUR SIDE

CHAPTER 25

A phrase I often repeat is that, whatever market we trade in, we should never forget the importance of having the odds for success on our side.

I return to this concept in this short chapter to show that when we do a proper analysis, when we have the odds of success on our side, we will close most of the trades in profit.

Here are two brief analyses I have written both on my website and TradingView account. I start with the analysis of Eur-Chf (<u>analysis made on April 24 2019</u>), followed by the Aud-Usd one on Aud-Usd.

"In the last weeks, CHF (Swiss Franc) has been very weak against all the major currencies. Most likely there is more than one reason for it, including the SNB (Swiss National Bank) that has sold Swiss Francs and bought Euros (as it has often done in the last four and a half years).

Today I analyse Eur-Chf because it has reached an interesting level. Below we can see the daily chart (figure 60).

Figure 60 - Eur-Chf daily chart (TradingView.com)

Two aspects are shown in the chart. The first, the price has reached an important area of resistance (1.14700/1.15000) that will hardly break easily.

The second, the 1.13600 level (approximately), the price of Eur-Chf on March 7, the day Draghi announced a new TLTRO for September during the ECB meeting.

The TLTRO (Targeted Longer-Term Refinancing Operations) which is the loan of money by the ECB to the credit sector (banks) at particularly favourable conditions, lasting four years to alleviate the problems of collection of European banks and support loans to families and businesses.

In other words, different names (Quantitative Easing and TLTRO) but the

179

same type of operation (loans non-repayable to banks). Yes, because I strongly doubt that at the end of the four years, the banks will repay the loan.

All this translates into greater liquidity on the markets and, therefore, depreciation of the Euro. And if in the short-term it is the speculation that moves a currency pair, in the medium to long-term they are the fundamentals that decide the right exchange rate. For this reason, in the coming weeks we will see a return of Eur-Chf, as the first target, in the 1.12000 area.

There would be the possibility for making a speech about CHF as a safe-haven currency in times of crisis, but given the trend of Wall Street and the new highs reached (Nasdaq) or about to be reached (S&P 500), it would still be a premature speech. However, selling Eur-Chf to cover the upward investment in equities and balancing the portfolio could be a wise idea."

In this case, the TLTRO was a strong signal of a future weakening of the Euro. Furthermore, the macroeconomic resistance that formed with the announcement was just below an area of resistance, which was broken in the past, only after the announcement by Draghi of the end of Quantitative Easing.

If we add that Eur-Chf is also used as a cover for other operations, including equities (and Wall Street was headed towards a new absolute high at that period), the odds of success in the trade were definitely on my side.

Below, we can see the same chart about three months later (figure 61).

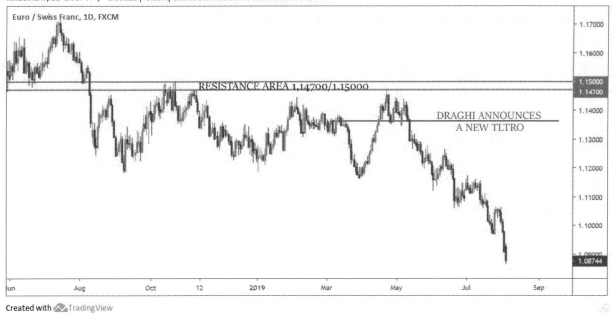

Figure 61 - Eur-Chf daily chart (TradingView.com)

In the following weeks, Eur-Chf started a bearish trend, going even beyond the second target of my trade to 1,10000.

You can read the analysis on TradingView (https://www.tradingview.com/chart/EURCHF/wa3ZxMi8-Eur-Chf-Analysis).

Now, let's see the next example, Aud-Usd (<u>analysis made on 3 July 2019</u>).

"On July 2, the Reserve Bank of Australia (RBA) cuts rates for the second time in 4 weeks. The first time had been on June 4.

The AUD situation is very interesting; I will analyse the currency pair Aud-Usd in order to try and describe a future scenario. Below we can see the daily chart (figure 62).

Figure 62 - Aud-Usd daily chart (TradingView.com)

The two blue lines highlight the two Australian interest rate cuts, while the two black put in evidence a support/resistance area (0.70250/0.70500).

The current price might be an excellent level to sell Aud-Usd, but there is an aspect to take into account. That is the ideal moment for gold which has reached $ 1,440 for the second time (double top?).

The Australian economy is "very sensitive" to gold, so a continuation of the appreciation of the yellow metal could push speculators to buy the Australian dollar.

Thus, we cannot exclude a break of Aud-Usd of the resistance because, in the short-term, the currencies follow the speculation. But for sure, this would represent (with the right market entry) an excellent opportunity to sell the currency pair (excess of price).

My strategy is the following: I start to sell Aud-Usd, using only a part of the position, in the area 0.70250. That is what I call the "spy-order." Usually, I use for the spy-order 1/4 of the whole position (never more than 1/3).

If the price rebounds on the resistance and then falls, even if it does with a little position, I am nonetheless inside the trade. In case Aud-Usd breaks the resistance, I have 3/4 of the position to use for selling the currency pair at a better level, with a lower risk."

If the first decision by the Reserve Bank of Australia to cut interest rates was already priced into the market, the second was less obvious, at least after such a short time.

To this, we have to add that the currency pair has reached a zone of technical resistance, even though less strong than the one seen on the Eur-Chf chart. However, the situation was not so strongly on my side as in the previous example.

A little later, even the United States would have decided to cut interest rates by 25 basis points and, not having the crystal ball, I did not know how much this would have affected (although all analysts foresaw it) on Aud-Usd.

If Fed Chairman Powell, in the speech following the communication of the decision taken, had hinted that there would be further rate cuts during the year, Aud-Usd would have jumped well beyond the resistance zone.

Hence, the decision to enter only with the spy-order, and to wait for the FOMC meeting before making further decisions.

Below, we can see the Aud-Usd daily chart a month later (figure 63).

Figure 63 - Aud-Usd daily chart (TradingView.com)

After a new test of the resistance area (that Aud-Usd also succeeded to break), the currency pair began a sharp decline. In this case, I had only opened the spy-order, but I could not regret my decision as I know I acted correctly and according to my trading plan.

There was a chance that the Aud-Usd could continue to rise for a while (speculation, FOMC meeting...), and I did not want to be in trouble if this scenario materialised.

You can read the analysis on TradingView (https://www.tradingview.com/chart/AUDUSD/OqdiR5Rp-AUD-RBA-cuts-rates-twice-in-4-weeks).

As we have seen, having the odds on our side allows us to work serenely and profitably. Organising everything, with a proper trading plan, will enable you to proceed with your business activity peacefully.

And that's all. In the next chapter, you will read my conclusions and a brief summary of everything you saw in this book.

FINAL COMMENTS

CHAPTER 26

Forex is not only a means to an end (make money with currencies) but something bigger that involves our entire portfolio. A macroeconomic reading teaches us the correct way to read the market and manage our portfolio. These concepts will not only come in handy in Forex but in all markets.

A correct reading of the market tells us how we are moving and gives us a statistical advantage. I do not mean that we will always achieve our goals, but we have an advantage: we know where we are, and we know what we are doing.

We always have to try to buy strength and sell weakness. Let's buy a weak currency against a potentially strong one just to make better use of short-term expectations (as we have seen with the analysis of Gbp-Usd). That is the basis of the analysis system. We must not invent anything; we have to note the data and assess the situation.

We must not attempt to anticipate the market or try to predict something according to our own personal views; we must always read only the real situation of a currency pair. Patience is the virtue of the trader. We wait for the right time, and we open a trade when there is an excess in price, when the odds of success are on our side, and, therefore, when it is easier for us to get a profit. A premature market entry, although not quite like flipping a coin, nonetheless reduces a lot our odds.

We are not gamblers when we open a trade, and therefore we shouldn't try any tricks that would be out of our control. We are investors, and investors must always put their money in the market when it has a statistical advantage, not when there is a 50/50 chance of success. This is because, if we aspire to this percentage, we might as well go and bet on red or blacks at the roulette table. It is in this regard that you must take the extra steps to differentiate yourself.

We cannot trade without uncertainty, but taking these steps gives us a higher probability for success. If there are no conditions, we remain outside of the market because we have to work much more in terms of statistic. We have to respect the market.

Let's keep in mind that it is not an indicator on a Metatrader (or other) platform that moves the markets in the short-term, but emotions. If, for example, you look at panic selling, all the indicators are in the oversold zone, but the market continues to fall. If we want to work with high percentages, we have to work only in certain specific situations.

As I have explained, I like to work on the price excess, because when the price is misaligned with the macroeconomy, I will get an increase in odds of success. Obviously, the certainty is never 100%, but in the long run, this will give me a profit, if I have followed my trading plan to the letter.

The market invites you to enter, especially when you spend a lot of time in front of the monitor, therefore, whether out of boredom or other factors, a trader tends to trade. A real trader, one that regularly gets a profit, is one who enters the market when he wants, at the price he wants.

I know that it is not easy because we are emotionally involved, we get carried away by our feelings, and this sometimes brings us to lose a good occasion to trade. However, this is the right way that will give us long-term survival in the markets and the ability to do very well with excellent profits.

And this is when we must watch our behaviour. That is what makes the difference, especially in the long-term.

This is why it is often said that, if we can see the situation calmly, we can also manage it effectively. We decide what to do, the market does not force us to do anything. We manage the situation as we planned and become masters of our trade, and not only that. By doing so, we often go in the wake of investment banks, essentially distancing ourselves from the mass.

Everything you have seen in this book is not suitable for "all the seasons", because you always have to evaluate the historical moment in which you are in. In particular situations, it is not unusual to see movements, in short to medium term, that are completely illogical.

That is what has been happening in the markets since the end of February 2020 with the "Covid-19" crisis. Everything seems crazy. Any connection with fundamentals and reality evaporates like a mist hit by the sun when markets collide with the general hysteria of traders, or the need to recover heavy losses from Hedge Funds. Everything loses meaning.

So, do not be surprised if you see the S&P 500 index collapse, and Usd-Jpy rise as shown in the chart in figure 64, in periods like this, this can also happen. After all, it is not an ordinary financial crisis, but the result of a pandemic.

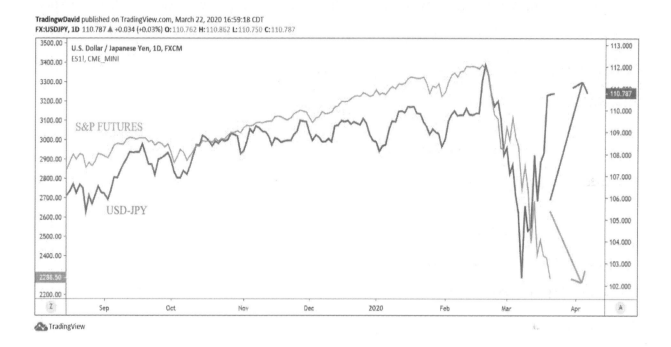

Figure 64 - S&P Futures and Usd-Jpy daily chart (TradingView.com)

My last tip: markets do not give away money. So, if there are situations that lead you to think so, be very careful.

In conclusion, you have seen the <u>four steps to analyse a currency pair correctly</u>, in order to understand which of the two currencies, and therefore economies, is the strongest.

You have seen how <u>in the medium to long-term, the Forex market is</u>

manipulated by central banks, and how to put yourself in a position to have the odds of success on your side. However, in the short-term is the speculation that moves the market.

For this reason, you must never anticipate market entry. You are better off losing a winning trade than finding yourself attempting, with difficulty, to manage a losing trade because you opened a position too hastily. Use the subjective probability to select the best trade entries.

Finally, forget technical analysis. It is not because of this that you will earn in Forex (and in trading in general) consistently. Professional traders do not use technical analysis.

This book is coming to an end; now, all you have to do is practice and gain experience. I understand that what I have tried to explain in the simplest possible way is actually a series of complicated concepts - at least, to begin with.

Do not worry, with time and application you will get used to having a different vision of Forex. You will learn to trade the currencies not by following an indicator anymore, but by considering the fundamental aspects and analysing the two economies that make up a currency pair.

This is the ninth and final edition; from the first edition, four years have passed in which I have expanded and updated the book with new chapters and aspects related to the currency market, trying to convey all my experience.

I hope I have succeeded at least in part, and I hope that what you have read will help you to become an excellent Forex trader.

I would like to thank from the bottom of my heart Caroline for her efforts in proofreading this book into English, she was very kind and professional. You can contact her through her email: carolinewinter4@hotmail.com.

For any questions my email is info@tradingwithdavid.com. On my website https://tradingwithdavid.com you can find articles, analysis, books, and much more.

You can also follow me on:

- **Twitter**: https://twitter.com/tradingwdavid;
- **LinkedIn**: https://www.linkedin.com/in/davidcarli;
- **TradingView**: https://www.tradingview.com/u/TradingwDavid. All you have to do is sign up (for free) to follow me.

Do not go yet; one last thing to do.

If you enjoyed this book or found it useful, I would be very grateful if you would post a short review on Amazon. Your support does make a difference, and I read all the reviews personally so I can get your feedback and make this book even better.

Thanks in advance for your support! I really hope that what you have read will help you in your trading.

Happy Trading to you all!

APPENDIX

PIP VALUE

APPENDIX A

Below you can see the table with the pip value of the most traded currency pairs.

Currency Pair	Minimum Pip value (for 1,000 USD)
Aud-Cad	0.07087
Aud-Chf	0.10289
Aud-Jpy	0.09331
Aud-Nzd	0.05934
Aud-Usd	0.10

Cad-Chf	0.10289
Cad-Jpy	0.09331
Chf-Jpy	0.09331
Eur-Aud	0.06416
Eur-Cad	0.07087
Eur-Chf	0.10289
Eur-Gbp	0.12102
Eur-Jpy	0.09331
Eur-Nok	0.00978
Eur-Nzd	0.05934
Eur-Sek	0.01015
Eur-Usd	0.10
Gbp-Aud	0.06416

Gbp-Cad	0.07087
Gbp-Chf	0.10289
Gbp-Jpy	0.09331
Gbp-Nzd	0.05934
Gbp-Usd	0.10
Nzd-Cad	0.07087
Nzd-Chf	0.10289
Nzd-Jpy	0.09331
Nzd-Usd	0.10
Usd-Cad	0.07087
Usd-Chf	0.10289
Usd-Cnh	0.01402
Usd-Jpy	0.09331

Usd-Mxn	0.00417
Usd-Rub	0.00136
Usd-Sgd	0.07006
Usd-Try	0.01449
Usd-Zar	0.00538

Table 10 – Pip value (May 18, 2020)

The values in the table above as well as being in US Dollars (and therefore, only available to be used for accounts in that currency) may also undergo, even if mildly, variations over time. In order to have the values in other currencies (for example, EUR, JPY, AUD, etc.) and to update them periodically, you can use the tool available on **Myfxbook** website (https://www.myfxbook.com/en/forex-calculators/pip-calculator).

WEB RESOURCES

APPENDIX B

Below, summarised, are all the resources you have seen in this book and others as well.

WEBSITE	LINK
Free Platform	
TradingView	https://www.tradingview.com
ProRealTime	https://www.prorealtime.com
Central Banks	
United States	https://www.federalreserve.gov/

Canada	https://www.bankofcanada.ca/
Eurozone	https://www.ecb.europa.eu/home/html/index.en.html
Great Britain	https://www.bankofengland.co.uk/
Switzerland	https://www.snb.ch/en/
Japan	http://www.boj.or.jp/en/index.htm/
Australia	https://www.rba.gov.au/
New Zealand	https://www.rbnz.govt.nz/

Reports

Econ. Projections	federalreserve.gov/monetarypolicy/fomccalendars.htm
Non-Farm Payrolls	https://www.bls.gov/bls/newsrels.htm#OEUS
C.O.T. Report	https://www.cftc.gov

Financial Site	
Barchart	https://www.barchart.com
Finviz	https://www.finviz.com
Investing	https://www.investing.com

Follow me	
Website	https://tradingwithdavid.com
Twitter	https://twitter.com/tradingwdavid
LinkedIn	https://www.linkedin.com/in/davidcarli/
TradingView	https://www.tradingview.com/u/TradingwDavid/

Tools	
Pip Calculator	https://www.myfxbook.com/en/forex-calculators/pip-calculator

Resources	
Economic Calendar	https://tradingwithdavid.com/economic-calendar

Table 11 - Web resources

FOREX GLOSSARY

APPENDIX C

Aggregate Demand: the sum of government spending, personal consumption expenditures, and business expenditures.

Algorithmic Trading: is a system of executing trades automatically based on advanced mathematical models and formulae that are pre-defined, as opposed to a person manually executing the trade. It is also commonly known as automated trading.

Appreciation: a currency is said to "appreciate" when it strengthens in price in response to market demand.

Arbitrage: the purchase or sale of an instrument and simultaneous taking of an equal and opposite position in a related market, in order to take advantage of small price differentials between markets.

Around: dealer jargon used in quoting when the forward premium/discount is near parity. For example, "two-two around" would translate into 2 points to either side of the present spot.

Ask: the "sell" price, which is sometimes referred to as the offer or

Right-Hand Side. The other side of the price is called the "bid" price or the Left-Hand Side.

Asset Allocation: investment practice that divides funds among different markets to achieve diversification for risk management purposes and expected returns consistent with an investor's objectives.

Asset Class: put simply, the classification of an asset. Different types of asset are Foreign Exchange, Equities, Fixed Income and Commodities.

At Best: here you are asking for your trade to be dealt at the best rate available at that time.

Aussie: an abbreviation of 'Australian', referring specifically to the Australian Dollar when used in trading.

Away from the Market: when the current price is higher or lower than your order price it is described as "away from the market."

Back Office: the departments and processes related to the settlement of financial transactions.

Balance of Trade: the value of a country's exports minus its imports.

Bank Rate: the rate at which a central bank lends to members of its banking system.

Bar Charts: standard bar charts are commonly used to convey price activity into an easily readable chart. Usually, four elements make up a bar chart, the Open, High, Low, and Close for the trading session/time period. A price bar can represent any time-frame the user wishes, from 1 minute to 1 month. The total vertical length/height of the bar represents the entire trading range for the period. The top of the bar represents the highest price of the period, and the bottom of the bar represents the lowest price of the period. The Open is represented by a small dash to the left of the bar, and the Close for the session is a small dash to the right of the bar.

Base Currency: in general terms, the base currency is the currency in which an investor or issuer maintains its book of accounts. In the FX markets, the US Dollar is normally considered the 'base' currency for quotes, meaning that quotes are expressed as a unit of $1 per the other currency quoted in the pair. The primary exceptions to this rule are the British Pound, the Euro and the Australian Dollar.

Basis Point: often abbreviated to BPS, is shown as 1/100 of 1%, or 0.0001. That is most commonly applied when quoting interest rates and yield changes. For example, if interest rates are increased from 1.00% to 1.40%, it would be described to have risen by 40 basis points.

Bear: someone of the belief that prices are going to go down.

Bear Market: a market distinguished by declining prices.

Best-Efforts Basis: when a trader executes an order at the price that is next available when there is above average order flow.

Bid: the "buy" price which is sometimes referred to as the bid or Left-Hand Side. The other side of the price is called the "ask" price or the Right-Hand Side.

Bid/Ask Spread: the difference between the bid and offer price, and the most widely used measure of market liquidity.

Big Figure: the first few digits of a Forex rate tend to remain fairly static and these are referred to as the Big Figure. As an example, say for Eur-Usd where the current quote is 1.36782/762, the Big Figure would be 1.36.

Bollinger Bands: are a technical indicator developed by John Bollinger, commonly used by traders to analyse currency price. They are volatility bands based on standard deviation (SD) and placed above and below a moving average. The settings for the Bollinger Bands can be adjusted to suit the particular characteristics of the currency being analysed. The principal rule of the Bollinger Band is that the closer the prices move to the upper band, the more overbought the market, and the closer the prices move to the lower band, the more oversold the market. Technical traders often interpret the tightening of the bands as an early indication that the volatility is about to increase sharply.

Book: in a professional trading environment, a 'book' is the summary of a trader's or desk's total positions.

Break: when prices suddenly move outside a previous range.

Bretton Woods Agreement of 1944: an agreement that established fixed foreign exchange rates for major currencies, provided for central bank intervention in the currency markets, and pegged the price of gold at the US $35 per ounce. The agreement lasted until 1971 when President Nixon overturned the Bretton Woods agreement and established a floating exchange rate for the major currencies.

Broker: an individual or firm that acts as an intermediary, putting together buyers and sellers for a fee or commission. In contrast, a 'dealer' commits capital and takes one side of a position, hoping to earn a spread (profit) by closing out the position in a subsequent trade with another party.

Brokerage: a brokerage or broker is a company that will provide trading in exchange for either fees or commission.

Bull: someone of the belief that prices are going to go up.

Bull Market: a market distinguished by rising prices.

Bundesbank: Germany's Central Bank.

Buying/Selling: in the Forex market currencies are always priced in pairs; therefore, all trades result in the simultaneous buying of one currency and the selling of another. The objective of currency trading is to buy the currency that increases in value relative to the one you sold. If you have bought a currency and the price appreciates in value, then you must sell the currency back in order to lock in the profit.

Buying on Margin: is essentially buying on credit. So, if you execute a trade, only part of the total value of the trade is actually paid for. The part that is paid for is called margin, and the rest is borrowed and will have interest charged.

Buy Stop: this is an order that is used to either close out a short position or start a new long position above market and is usually placed above resistance levels.

Cable: trader jargon referring to the Sterling/US Dollar exchange rate.

So-called because the rate was originally transmitted via a transatlantic cable beginning in the mid-1800s.

Candlestick Chart: a chart that indicates the trading range for the day as well as the opening and closing price. If the open price is higher than the close price, the rectangle between the open and close price is shaded. If the close price is higher than the open price, that area of the chart is not shaded.

Central Bank: a government or quasi-governmental organisation that manages a country's monetary policy. For example, the US central bank is the Federal Reserve, and the German central bank is the Bundesbank. others include the ECB, BOE, BOJ.

Chartist: an individual who uses charts and graphs and interprets historical data to find trends and predict future movements. Also referred to as Technical Trader.

Choice Market: a market with no spread. All trades buys and sells occur at that one price.

Clearing: the process of settling a trade.

Contagion: the tendency of an economic crisis to spread from one market to another. In 1997, political instability in Indonesia caused high volatility in their domestic currency, the Rupiah. From there, the contagion spread to other Asian emerging currencies, and then to Latin America, and is now referred to as the 'Asian Contagion'.

Collateral: something given to secure a loan or as a guarantee of performance.

Commission: a transaction fee charged by a broker.

Contagion: the tendency of an economic crisis to spread from one market to another. In 1997, financial instability in Thailand caused high volatility in its domestic currency, the Baht, which triggered a contagion into other East Asian emerging currencies, and then to Latin America. It is now referred to as the Asian Contagion

Confirmation: a document exchanged by counterparts to a transaction that states the terms of said transaction.

Contract: the standard unit of trading.

Contract (Unit or Lot): the standard unit of trading on certain exchanges.

Counterparty: one of the participants in a financial transaction.

Country Risk: risk associated with a cross-border transaction, including but not limited to legal and political conditions such as war etc.

Cross Rates: a two-way price made up of one currency quoted against another currency that is not USD. The quote consists of the two individual exchange rates against the USD.

Currency: any form of money issued by a government or central bank and used as legal tender and a basis for trade.

Currency Pair: the two currencies that make up a foreign exchange rate. For example, Eur-Usd (Euro/U.S. Dollar).

Currency Risk: the probability of an adverse change in exchange rates.

Day Trader: speculators who take positions in commodities and then liquidate those positions prior to the close of the same trading day.

Day Trading: refers to positions which are opened and closed on the same trading day.

Dealer: an individual who acts as a principal or counterpart to a transaction. Principals take one side of a position, hoping to earn a spread (profit) by closing out the position in a subsequent trade with another party. In contrast, a broker is an individual or firm that acts as an intermediary, putting together buyers and sellers for a fee or commission.

Deficit: a negative balance of trade or payments.

Delivery: an FX trade where both sides make and take actual delivery of the currencies traded.

Depreciation: a fall in the value of a currency due to market forces.

Derivative: a contract that changes in value in relation to the price movements of a related or underlying security, futures or other physical instruments. An Option is the most common derivative instrument.

Devaluation: the deliberate downward adjustment of a currency's price, normally by official announcement.

Discretionary Account: an account where the customer gives someone else permission to make trading decisions for them.

Diversified Carry Basket: a portfolio of carrying trades that are spread out amongst different carry and funding currencies in an attempt to spread the risk and thus limit losses.

Dollar Index (DXY): the Dollar Index is an index of the Dollar's value against a basket of five major currencies: EUR, JPY, GBP, CAD, SEK and CHF. The weights of each currency in the index are not representative of US trade, so the DXY is not a particularly good measure of the Dollar's value. It is just a convenient way to take a position on the Dollar in general, instead of versus a specific currency. The DXY is an index of the Dollar against a basket of the currencies of several major trading partners of the US. It was originally created in 1973 by JP Morgan. Its components have only been rebalanced once, to take account of the introduction of the Euro. We offer a contract on the DXY. It is a convenient way to take a view on the movement of the Dollar in general, rather than the Dollar against one particular currency.

Dollar Rate: the amount of foreign currency quoted against one US Dollar.

Drawdown: the size of a drop in the value of an account from its peak to its low.

Easing: this term refers to either a small price fall in a currency or when a central bank takes action to try to encourage spending, for example, lowering interest rates.

Economic Indicator: such as GDP, foreign investment, and the trade balance reflect the general health of an economy and are therefore responsible for the underlying shifts in supply and demand for that currency.

End of Day Mark-to-Market: the value of a dealer's book at the end of the day based on the closing market prices. Any P&L is recorded at these rates.

End Of Day Order (EOD): an order to buy or sell at a specified price. This order remains open until the end of the trading day which is typically 5 pm EST.

Entity Trading Account: a trading account for a company as opposed to an individual with a designated person responsible for any trading decisions.

Escrow Account: a segregated account where customer money is kept separate from a dealer's operating funds.

Euro: since 2002 the Euro has been the currency of the European Monetary Union (EMU). A replacement for the European Currency Unit (ECU). Members of the EMU are Germany, France, Belgium, Luxembourg, Austria, Finland, Ireland, the Netherlands, Italy, Spain and Portugal.

Eurocurrency: a currency that is deposited in a financial institution located outside the currency's country of origin.

EuroDollar: US Dollars deposited in a bank outside the USA.

European Central Bank (ECB): the Central Bank for the new European Monetary Union.

Excess Margin Deposits: funds deposited in a trading account exceeding what is required in margin terms.

Exchange Control: this term refers to strategies used by central banks to prevent depletion of their foreign exchange reserves.

Exchange Rate: what one currency is worth against another. Currencies have a spot rate which refers to trades settled in two business days and a forward rate, which is the spot rate adjusted to show the interest rate differential between the two.

Execution: completing a trade.

Exit: this is essentially closing your position. So, if you are long, you will sell, and if you are short, you will buy.

Exotics: Exotic Currencies are those that are traded infrequently and in very small volumes in comparison to the major currencies. They are called such due to their rarity in the global market. Exotic Currencies are not as widely available for trade through normal brokerage accounts. They carry a contrasting set of characteristics to major currencies. They are, as a rule, less liquid and carry a considerably lower volume than major currencies. As such, they require less influence to cause a major wave. A trade that may carry no influence on a major pair may carry a greater influence on an exotic pair as there is less volume in and out to dilute the trade in that particular market. Trading an exotic currency can be expensive, as the bid-ask spread is usually large, they are potentially hostile and more volatile than major pairs.

Exposure: the net of all long and short positions for a particular currency. Based on the trader's positions for all currencies, his/her exposures can result in either loss or gain.

Fast Market: when prices move particularly quickly, often meaning that trades cannot be executed fast enough.

Federal Deposit Insurance Corporation (FDIC): the regulatory agency responsible for administering bank depository insurance in the US.

Federal Reserve: the central bank of the United States, with responsibility for implementing the country's monetary policy and regulating member banks of the System. The Fed was created in 1913 and is composed of 12 regional Federal Reserve Banks and a national Board of Governors.

Fibonacci Technical Study: the Fibonacci Fans and Bands are three-line guides drawn onto charts. They are derived from the Fibonacci number sequence, discovered by Leonardo Fibonacci. This sequence is written as follows: 1, 1, 2, 3, 5, 8, 13, 21, 34, 55... Infinitely, where the next number is equal to the sum of the two previous. Each number to the next has a ratio of .618, whilst each alternating number has a ratio of .382. Interestingly, these add up to 1, and the halfway point of the two is .50. Therefore, .382, .50, and .618 are the three numbers used for calculating the aforementioned lines, which some traders believe can be used to pinpoint areas of support and resistance.

Fixed Exchange Rate: official rate set by monetary authorities for one or more currencies.

Flat/square: dealer jargon used to describe a position that has been completely reversed, e.g. you bought $500,000 then sold $500,000, thereby creating a neutral (flat) position.

Flexible Exchange Rate: an exchange rate that is fixed, but is re-evaluated frequently.

Floating Exchange Rates: floating exchange rates refer to the value of a currency is decided by supply and demand.

Foreign Exchange: (Forex, FX) is the simultaneous buying of one currency while selling for another. This market of exchange has more buyers and sellers and daily volume than any other in the world. Taking place in the major financial institutions across the globe, the Forex market is open 24-hours a day.

Forward: the pre-specified exchange rate for a foreign exchange contract settling at some agreed future date, based upon the interest rate differential between the two currencies involved.

Forward Contract: a forward contract fixes the exchange rate for future delivery at a date to be agreed by both participants. A deposit (or a minimum margin) is usually required in forwarding transactions. For example, if I want to lock in today's rate to buy $10,000 at 1.5820 Canadian for the next 4 months, I will have the ability to purchase up to $10,000 at this rate.

Forward Points: the pips added to or subtracted from the current exchange rate to calculate a forward price.

Forward Rates (Swaps): a Forward Rate refers to a cash price of 2 currencies interest difference for a fixed term. Forward rates can be calculated easily given the fixed term interest rates of each currency and the current spot rate.

Forward Trading: forward trading is making the opposite trade of a spot trade in a given period of time. Often investors will swap their trades forward for anywhere from a week or two up to several months depending on the time-frame of the investment. Even though a forward trade is on a future date, the position can be closed out at any time. The closing part of the position is then swapped forward to the same future value date.

Fundamental Analysis: focuses on the economic forces of supply and demand that cause price movement. The Fundamentalist studies the causes of market movement, whereas the Technician studies the effects.

Futures Contract: an obligation to exchange a good or instrument at a set price on a future date. The primary difference between a Future and a Forward is that Futures are typically traded over an exchange (Exchange-Traded Contacts – ETC), versus forwards, which are considered Over The Counter (OTC) contracts. An OTC is any contract NOT traded on an exchange.

Gearing: also known as margin trading. A term used in the relationship between actual equity versus controlling equity.

Golden Cross: the point at which two moving averages intersect, which is generally considered to be a good sign that the underlying currency will move in the same direction.

Goldilocks Economy: was a term coined back in the mid-1902 to describe an economy that was not too hot and not too cold. That typically describes an economy that enjoyed steady growth with the nominal rate of inflation.

Good 'til Cancelled (GTC): an order to buy or sell at a specified price. This order remains open until filled or until the client cancels.

Good 'til Date: an order to buy or sell at a specified price that will expire on a specific date. If the order has not been executed by the expiry date, the order will be cancelled.

Hard Currency: a currency that investors have confidence in. Examples could be the US Dollar or the Euro.

Head and Shoulders: a price trend pattern which has three peaks, the middle one higher than the surrounding two forming what looks to be a head with two shoulders on either side. This pattern is seen as an indicator of a trend reversal. The left shoulder is typically formed at the end of an extensive move where volume is noticeably high. Once the left shoulder is formed, the market reacts and price slides. When price recovers, it rallies up to form a peak at the head greater than the peak of the left shoulder. Price then reacts down again to form a second trough. The right shoulder is formed when prices move up again, but to a level lower than the peak of the head and then fall to below the peak of the left shoulder at the very least. A neckline is formed by connecting the lowest points of the two troughs. The slope of this line can either be up or down depending on the depth of each trough, respectively. When the slope is down a more reliable signal.

Hedging: a hedging transaction is a purchase or sale of a financial product, having as its purpose the elimination of loss arising from price fluctuations. With regards to currency transactions, it would protect one against fluctuations in the foreign exchange rate. (see Forward Contract).

High/Low: refers to the daily traded high and low price.

IFEMA: acronym for International Foreign Exchange Master Agreement.

Indicative Quote: a price quoted by a market maker as an indicator rather than a definite price.

Inflation: an economic condition whereby prices for consumer goods rise, eroding purchasing power.

Initial Margin: the initial deposit of collateral required to enter into a position as a guarantee of future performance.

Interbank Rates: the Foreign Exchange rates at which large international banks quote other large international banks.

Intraday Trading: positions that are opened and closed within the same trading day.

Key Currency: when smaller economies align their exchange rate to that of a more dominant currency, this latter currency is known as a key currency. For example, the Euro or US Dollar are both common key currencies.

Kiwi: trader's term for the New Zealand Dollar.

Leading Indicators: statistics that are considered to predict future economic activity.

Leading Side: if spot is going higher, the leading side of the price is the offer because it gets to the higher point first. If spot is going lower, the bid gets there first and is the leading side.

Left-Hand Side: the "buy" price which is sometimes referred to as the bid or Left-Hand Side. The other side of the price is called the "ask" price or the Right-Hand Side.

Leverage: by definition, leverage is "the exertion of force by means of a lever or an object used in the manner of a lever." In financial terms, the 'lever' can mean to reinvest debt in an effort to earn a greater return than the cost of interest. When a firm uses a considerable proportion of debt to finance its investments, it is considered highly leveraged. In the world of Forex, this leaver is borrowed capital or margin. The greater the value of leverage, the greater the ratio of margin to the maximum position size. With a deposit of $ 5000 and a leverage of 50, a trader could enter a position with a face value of $ 250,000. Leveraging allows you to profit quickly, but lose money just as fast. See also Margin.

Liability: the obligation to deliver the currency as part of a spot transaction. In speculative Forex trading, the currency is not delivered. All profits and losses are added to or subtracted from margin deposits.

LIBOR: the London Inter-Bank Offered Rate. Banks use LIBOR when borrowing from another bank.

Limit order: an order with restrictions on the maximum price to be paid or the minimum price to be received. As an example, if the current price of Usd-Jpy is 102.00/05, then a limit order to buy USD would be at a price below 102. (i.e. 101.50).

Limit Price: the specified price as part of a limit order.

Line Charts: the Line Chart connects single prices for a selected time period.

Liquid: the term used where there are large supply and demand for a particular asset, which usually means that spreads are tight and availability is plentiful. The opposite of this is illiquid markets, whereby there is less availability and subsequently spreads tend to be wider.

Liquidation: the closing of an existing position through the execution of an offsetting transaction.

Liquidity: the ability of a market to accept large transaction with minimal to no impact on price stability.

Long position: a position that appreciates in value if market prices increase. When one buys a currency, their position is long.

Lots: one standard lot in the FX market is 100,000 units of the base currency. That would mean €100,000 of Eur-Usd, $100,000 of Usd-Jpy, etc. There are also **mini-lots** of 10,000 units and **micro-lots** of 1,000 units. A micro-lot is usually the smallest available unit for trading.

Majors: refers to the major currencies that are traded: USD, EUR, GBP, CHF, AUD, CAD, NZD, and JPY. Also known as Principals.

Managed Float: a "deposit" that is made as collateral towards the total amount of trade.

Margin: is a percentage of the total value of a transaction. It is the collateral payment made by a trader to secure leverage. For example, if a trader places a £ 1000 margin for the control of £ 10,000, their leverage would be 10:1 as they are now in control of ten times their initial payment. Therefore, in this instance, the margin would be 10%.

Margin Account: an account that lets you trade on credit.

Margin Call: is made when your account is in deficit. To avoid liquidation, positions will need to be either closed or reduced or alternatively, additional funds will need to be added to the account. Note: In a fast-moving market, there may be little time between margin alerts, or there may not be sufficient time to receive the warning. It is very important for individuals to proactively manage the status of their accounts.

Margin Requirement: the minimum collateral that is needed on an account before executing a trade.

Mark-To-Market: the process of re-evaluating all open positions with the current market prices. These new values then determine margin requirements.

Market Maker: someone who "makes a market" or who provides two-way quotes against which they are either willing to buy or sell. Market makers earn their money from the spread on a price – the difference between the bid and offer price.

Market Order: an order for immediate execution at the best available price.

Market Risk: the risk associated with investing in the market. For example, high volatility often translates into high risk. Occasionally, market risk is also known as systematic risk.

Maturity: the date for settlement or expiry of a trade.

Mid: the price halfway between the bid and ask quote offered by dealers. For example, if the bid is 1.4426 and the ask is 1.4430, the mid-price is 1.4428.

Moving Average: method of smoothing out data on price charts so that trends are easier to spot. Average refers to a mathematical average or a statistical mean that is plotted over the original curve.

Narrow Market: also referred to as a thin market, where there is light trading, low liquidity, high volatility and high spreads. That is the polar opposite.

Net Account Value: this is your overall account balance, so all your cash plus or minus any unrealised profit or losses.

Net Position: currency positions that have not yet been offset with opposite positions.

News Trader: an investor who bases his/her decisions on the outcome of a news announcement and its impact on the market.

Non-Farm Payrolls (NFP): this figure is released on the first Friday of every month and represents the total number of paid workers of any business, excluding farm, general government, private household and non-profit organisations that provide assistance to individuals employees in the United States. The NFP report also contains estimates of the averages of the workweek and weekly earnings of all Non-Farm employees.

Offer: the "sell" price, which is sometimes referred to as the ask price or Right-Hand Side. The other side of the price is called the "bid" price or the Left-Hand Side.

Options: these are tradable contracts giving the right, but not obligation, to buy or sell currencies at a future date and a prearranged price. Options are used to hedge against adverse price movements or to speculate against price rises or falls. Trading options is riskier than trading spot currency but offers potentially higher returns.

Order: an instruction to buy or sell a specified amount at a specified rate, which remains valid until the trade is completed or until a time that is stated. The two most common types of orders are limit and Stop-loss orders.

Oscillators: an Oscillator is in effect, the measurement of an object be it physical, graphical or data, that moves back and forth between two given points. The movement is called oscillation, and at all times, this will occur between the two given points. In Forex, Oscillators are Technical Analysis tools that provide buy and sell signals, characterised by a signal that oscillates between overbought and oversold levels. Examples of different Oscillators in Forex would be, The Stochastic, Parabolic SAR, and Relative Strength Index (RSI). Each of these is designed to signal a possible reversal where the price is ready to change direction. Oscillators are also often known as Leading Indicators.

Over The Counter (OTC): refers to trading that is not done over a formal exchange. Traditional Forex is traded over the counter, meaning traders entered into Forex transactions with another counterparty rather than through an exchange.

Overbought: a currency pair is overbought when its price rises much more quickly than usual in response to net buying. Once overbought, the pair is then expected to make a contrarian move, meaning its price is expected to fall.

Overnight: trades that extend past the current trade day into the next.

Oversold: a currency pair is oversold when its price falls much more quickly than usual, declining too far in response to net selling. Once oversold, the pair is then expected to make a contrarian move, meaning its price is expected to rise.

Pip: The word 'pip' is an acronym for 'percentage in point.' The term has historically referred to the smallest incremental movement in price in the currencies trading market. The majority of currency pairs were quoted to four decimal places, so the smallest pip movement was that of the fourth decimal place. For example, if Eur-Usd rose from 1.3975 to 1.3977, it had risen two pips. There were some exceptions. The Japanese Yen (JPY) was priced to just two decimal places so a currency pair with JPY as the quote currency would have a pip equal to 0.01. A move in Usd-Jpy of 128.50 to 128.51 was one pip. In 2005 we were instrumental in introducing an additional decimal point to pricing in the interbank market.

Political Risk: exposure to changes in governmental policy which will have an adverse effect on an investor's position.

Position: the netted total holdings of a given currency.

Premium: in the currency markets, describes the amount by which the forward or futures price exceed the spot price.

Price: the cost of purchasing a second currency in terms of a first currency.

Price Transparency: describes quotes to which every market participant has equal access.

Profit/Loss or "P&L": the actual "realised" gain or loss resulting from trading activities on closed Positions, plus the theoretical "unrealised" gain or loss on open positions that have been Mark-to-Market.

Quantitative Easing: the act of a country's central bank increasing the amount of money in the economy at a time when interest rates are very low as a way of increasing economic growth.

Quote: an indicative market price, normally used for information purposes only.

Rally: a recovery in price after a period of decline.

Range: the difference between the highest and lowest price of a currency pair during a given trading period.

Rate: the price of one currency in terms of another, typically used for dealing purposes.

Re-quotes: occur when you place an "at the market" order and find that your order was filled, or executed, at a different price than what had appeared on the screen at the time you place your order. Sometimes this is unavoidable, as when the market is moving quite quickly, and the price has changed in the few seconds between your pressing the button and the broker executing your trade. But sometimes it is not unavoidable at all; sometimes unscrupulous brokers put attractive prices up on their screens in order to win business, but then execute incoming trades at prices that are more advantageous to them.

Resistance: a term used in technical analysis indicating a specific price level at which analysis concludes people will sell.

Retail FX Market: comprises a wide range of non-institutional traders, from large organisations to individual investors.

Revaluation: an increase in the exchange rate for a currency as a result of central bank intervention. Opposite of Devaluation.

Revaluation Rates: the revaluation rates are the market rates used when a trader runs an end-of-day to establish profit and loss for the day.

Right Hand Side: refers to the Ask or Offer price. That is the price at which traders buy.

Risk: exposure to uncertain change, the variability of returns significantly the likelihood of less-than-expected returns.

Risk Capital: the amount of money that an individual can afford to invest, which, if lost would not affect their lifestyle.

Risk Management: to hedge one's risk they will employ financial analysis and trading techniques.

Roll-Over: the process whereby the settlement of a deal is rolled forward to another value date. The cost of this process is based on the interest rate differential of the two currencies.

Rollover Rate: the daily rollover interest rate is the amount a trader either pays or earns, depending on the established margin and position in the market. To avoid rollovers simply make sure positions are closed at the established end of the market day.

Scalping: is a form of extremely short-term trading. Scalpers frequently trade, going both long and short a currency pair, with the aim of making many small profits on intraday moves. Scalpers often try to profit from the increase in volatility that occurs when major economic indicators are released.

Sell Limit Order: an order to enter a position only at a specified price (the limit) or higher.

Sell Stop: a limit order with a limit placed below the current market price. Once triggered, the limit order becomes a market order.

Selling Short: selling a currency pair that involves being short the base currency and long the quote currency, with the intent of buying the currency pair at a later time when prices are lower in order to make a profit.

Settlement: the process by which a trade is finalised and entered into the books and records of the counterparts to a transaction, normally two business days after the trade.

Short: selling a currency, with the intent of buying it at a later time when prices are lower in order to make a profit.

Short Position: an investment position that benefits from a decline in market price. When one sells a currency, their position is short.

Slippage: occurs when you place an order to be filled at a specified rate, but it is filled at a different rate than you requested. For example, you might be long EUR/USD overnight with a stop-loss order to sell your position if it falls to a certain level, but find when you wake up that the market went through that level and you were stopped out at a worse level than you wanted, thereby losing more money than you had budgeted for.

Spike: when a price moves unexpectedly.

Spot: a currency deposit transaction or the simultaneous purchase and sale of a currency, or vice versa by means of swap for spot value day against the next working day.

Spot Price: the current market price. Settlement of spot transactions usually occurs within two business days.

Spot (Rate): in FX Markets, Spot refers to the cash price without interest factored in.

Spot Trade: when you trade foreign exchange, you are always quoted a spot price 2 business days in advance. That is under normal conditions where there are no bank holidays in the traded currencies countries or is not over a weekend.

Spread: the difference between the bid (buy) and offer (ask, sell) prices; in other words, the spread is the commission that the brokerage house makes on each trade. That can vary widely between currencies and between brokerage firms. For example, Usd-Jpy may bid at 131.40 and ask at 131.45, this five-pip spread defines the trader's cost, which can be recovered with a favourable currency move in the market.

Square: purchase and sales of currencies are in balance, and thus, the trader has no open position.

Sterling: slang for British Pound.

Stop-loss: order type whereby an open position is automatically liquidated at a specific price, often used to minimise exposure to losses if the market moves against an investor's position. As an example, if an investor is long USD at 156.27, they might wish to put in a stop-loss order for 155.49, which would limit losses should the dollar depreciate, possibly below 155.49.

Stop-loss Strategy: a trading strategy that involves setting limit orders at different price levels to avoid incurring further losses.

Stochastic Oscillator: this technical analysis indicator is based on the premise that during an upward trading market, prices tend to close near their highs, and during a downward trading market, prices tend to close near their lows.

Strike Price: the price at which the underlying asset can be bought or sold as specified in an option contract.

Support Levels: a term used in technical analysis indicating a specific price level at which a currency will have the inability to cross below. Recurring failure for the price to move below that point produces a pattern that can usually be shaped by a straight line. It is the opposite of Resistance levels.

Swap: a currency swap is the simultaneous sale and purchase of the same amount of a given currency at a forward exchange rate.

Swap Price: a price adjustment, added to the opening price of the position, for forwarding a Forex trade beyond the original value date. It is a function of the interest rate differential between the two trading currencies and can be in your favour or against you.

Swift: Society of Worldwide Interbank Financial Telecommunications. It is a dedicated computer network that is set up to support fund transfer messages between member banks worldwide.

Swissy: another name for the Swiss Franc.

Take Profit: a limit order that is placed above the market with a long position or below the market with a short position. When the market reaches the limit price, the position is closed thereby locking in a profit.

Technical Analysis: an effort to forecast prices by analysing market action through chart study, volume, trends, moving averages, patterns, formations and many other technical indicators.

Technical Correction: a price adjustment based on technical factors like resistance and support levels, as well as overbought and oversold levels, instead of market sentiment.

Technical Indicators: short-term trends that technical analysts use to predict future price movements of securities and commodities. Also called technicals, technicalities.

Tick: minimum price move.

Ticker: shows a current and recent history of a currency either in the format of a graph or table.

Tomorrow Next (Tom/Next): simultaneous buying and selling of a currency for delivery the following day.

Trade Date: the date on which a position is opened.

Trading: buying or selling of goods and services among countries called commerce. Forex Trading is the trading of Foreign Currencies.

Trailing Side: if spot is going higher the trailing side of the price is the bid if spot is going lower the offer is the trailing side.

Trailing Stop: a trailing stop-loss order is in effect a stop-loss order that follows your trade around and closes it out when the price has moved a certain amount from the highest level since the inception of the trade. Trailing stops are set in terms of the number of pips, not levels.

Transaction Cost: the cost of buying or selling a financial instrument.

Transaction Date: the date on which a trade occurs.

Trend: simply the direction of the market, usually broken down to three categories: major, intermediate and short-term trends. Three directions are also associated.

Trend Line: this is a Technical Analysis indicator, also called or linear regression, which is a statistical tool used to uncover trends. It is calculated by using the "Least Squares" method. There are two ways to use the linear regression line: a. Trade in the direction of the Trend line. b. Construct a parallel trend channel above and below the Trend line to be used as support and resistance levels.

Turnover: the total money value of all executed transactions in a given time period; volume.

Two-Way Price: when both a bid and offer rate is quoted for an FX transaction.

Unconvertible Currency: a currency that cannot be exchanged for another because of foreign exchange regulations.

Undervalued: when a currency is below its purchasing power parity it is considered undervalued.

Unit: a widely used quantity of currency.

Unrealised Profit/Loss (Unrealised P&L): a valuation of the current position and the resultant profit or loss if the position were to be liquidated at that moment. They become realised profits or losses when the position is closed.

Uptick: a new price quote at a price higher than the preceding quote.

Uptick Rule: in the U.S., a regulation whereby a security may not be sold short unless the last trade prior to the short sale was at a price lower than the price at which the short sale is executed.

Us Dollar: the currency of the United States of America.

US Prime Rate: the interest rate at which US banks will lend to their prime corporate customers.

Value Date: the date on which counterparts to a financial transaction agree to settle their respective obligations, i.e., exchanging payments. For spot currency transactions, the value date is normally two business days forward. Also known as the maturity date.

Variable Currency: in Forex, this is the currency that the investor pays with or receives when trading. For example, in Eur-Usd, the variable currency is USD, that is, one unit of EUR is worth a variable amount of USD. When you buy EUR, you pay with USD, and when you sell EUR you receive USD. The other currency (EUR in the example above) is called the base currency.

Variation Margin: funds a broker must request from the client to have the required margin deposited. The term usually refers to additional funds that must be deposited as a result of unfavourable price movements.

Volatility: a measure of price fluctuations. The standard deviation of a price series is commonly used to measure price volatility.

Volatility Index (VIX): shows the market's expectation of 30-day volatility. It is constructed using the implied volatilities of a wide range of S&P 500 index options. The VIX is a widely used measure of market risk and is often referred to as the "investor fear gauge."

Volume: represents the total amount of trading activity in a particular stock, commodity or index for that day. It is the total number of contracts traded during the day.

Weak Dollar/ Strong Dollar: Dollar is said to be weak (relative to a previous time period) against another currency when more Dollars are required to buy one unit of another currency. The Dollar is strong or has gained in strength when fewer Dollars are required to buy one unit of another currency. For example, if $ 1 buys 3 Swiss Franc in 1989, but today $ 1 buys only 1.5 Swiss Franc then the Dollar has weakened against CHF.

Whipsaw: slang for a condition of a highly volatile market where a sharp price movement is quickly followed by a sharp reversal.

Working Day: when the banks in the country of origin for a particular currency are open for business. For currency pairs, this is compounded by the fact that both banks must be open.

Yard: slang for a billion.

YIELD: return on capital investment.

Made in the USA
Las Vegas, NV
19 February 2021